WWF for a living planet®

ANDHRA PRADESH NATURAL HERITAGE SERIES

The Common Birds and Mammals of Andhra Pradesh

Illustrated by
Sachin Jaltare

Universities Press

Universities Press (India) Private Limited

Registered Office
3-6-747/1/A & 3-6-754/1, Himayatnagar, Hyderabad 500 029 (A.P.) India
email: info@universitiespress.com

Distributed by
Orient Blackswan Private Limited

Registered Office
3-6-752 Himayatnagar, Hyderabad 500 029 (A.P.) India

Other Offices
Bangalore / Bhopal / Bhubaneshwar / Chennai
Ernakulam / Guwahati / Hyderabad / Jaipur / Kolkata
Lucknow / Mumbai / New Delhi / Patna

First published 2009

ISBN 978 81 7371 653 9

Set in Times New Roman 10/12 by
Sigma Publishing Services, Chennai, India

Printed by
Graphica Printers, Hyderabad 500 013

Published by
Universities Press (India) Private Limited
3-6-747/1/A & 3-6-754/1, Himayatnagar, Hyderabad 500 029 (A.P.) India.
and
World Wide Fund for Nature-India
Andhra Pradesh State Office (APSO)
818, Castle Hills, Rd. No. 2, Vijaynagar Colony
Hyderabad 500 057

CONTENTS

Dr. Y.S. RAJASEKHARA REDDY

HYDERABAD

9.8.2008

CHIEF MINISTER
ANDHRA PRADESH

I am glad that the Andhra Pradesh State Office of WWF-India is coming out with a book on the common birds and mammals of Andhra Pradesh.

In Andhra Pradesh, the diversity of flora and fauna is distinct to different parts of the state, as it is endowed with some of the most exquisite fauna. Distinct cultural and geographic features of Andhra, Rayalseema and Telangana regions make the state rich in biodiversity much to the delight of any admirer or ecotourist. We have bird sanctuaries at Kolleru, Manjira and Neelapattu, strengthening the ecotourism of the state.

Awareness and aptitude to watch and study birds and mammals will ultimately help promote travel and tourism in a big way.

I hope that thc narrative description and hand painted illustrations of this book compiled by WWF would contribute to environmental conservation and protection in Andhra Pradesh.

(Y. S. RAJASEKHARA REDDY)

Dr. (Mrs.) J. GEETA REDDY
Minister for Tourism, Sugar Major Industries, Commerce & Export Promotions

HYDERABAD
29.07.2008

MESSAGE

In our hectic lives, where all our energy is spent in earning our daily bread and living in artificial, polluted environs, surrounded by technology and artificial intelligence, we hardly find time to relax, unwind and smell the flowers in the glory of nature.

There is much more to our State than what meets the eye. Andhra Pradesh is not only about booming cities, glorious temples and ancient monuments; it also has superb natural locales and hidden biodiversity havens. AP has tremendous potential for Ecotourism catering to tourists from not only the state but also from other states of India and abroad.

This book the common birds and mammals of Andhra Pradesh, brought out by WWF-India is an attempt to open our eyes to the kaleidoscope of creatures in the natural world around us. The lucid style, attractive pictures and nuggets of information in this book make a wonderful read and draw readers to explore their surroundings.

I commend WWF-India, APSO for coming up with this interesting and wholesome book that covers both common mammals and common birds of the state. I hope many more such books are brought out in the future.

(Dr. J. GEETA REDDY)

SATRUCHARLA VIJAYARAMARAJU
Minister for forests, Environment, Science and Technology & Minor Irrigation

HYDERABAD

29.07.2008

MESSAGE

I am very happy to know that WWF's Andhra Pradesh State Office is bringing out a book on the birds and mammals commonly found in our state. Our biodiversity is under constant threat from overexploitation of natural resources beyond the land's carrying capacity and heavy human and livestock pressure on our forests.

The effort of WWF, A.P. State Office in bringing out this beautiful book is laudable. I hope that readers will develop a fondness for nature and wilderness areas of our state and will come forward to help restore our fragile ecosystems.

(SATRUCHARLA VIJAYA RAMA RAJU)

MESSAGE FROM MR. JAMSHYD GODREJ

I congratulate WWF India's AP State Office for bringing out a field guide on the common birds and mammals of Andhra Pradesh. This book covers two very interesting and eye-catching components of the natural heritage of this state- namely birds and mammals. Linked with these is relevant information on protected areas and active organisations dedicated to wildlife conservation. The book's lively illustrations and interesting write-ups will certainly draw the readers to this picturesque and richly diverse landscape of Andhra Pradesh.

I wish the WWF team members in Andhra Pradesh good luck with this book, and hope that they will bring out more books in this series in future.

Jamshyd N. Godrej
(President, WWF-India)

WWF® for a living planet®

WWF-India Secretariat :
Pirojsha Godrej National
Conservation Centre
172-B, Lodi Estate,
New Delhi-110 003
India

Tel: +011-51504815-18
Fax: +011-51504795/79
www.wwfindia.org

Ravi Singh
Secretary General & CEO

MESSAGE

WWF-India has been working in India since 1969 and in Andhra Pradesh since 1972 to protect the State's natural environment and to build a future in which humans live in harmony with nature.

Awareness of our surroundings plays a crucial role in encouraging conservation. This book on Andhra Pradesh's Natural Heritage describing common birds and mammals carries forward this theme most effectively through coloured illustrations and engaging write-ups. The description of the various protected areas in the book will surely encourage readers to visit some of these wilderness areas, explore and appreciate the various aspects of nature.

It is commendable that the Andhra Pradesh State Office has added another informative publication to WWF's list of nature publications. I hope that this book will open a whole new world of experience to its readers.

Ravi Singh

WWF *for a living planet*®

WWF-INDIA
Andhra Pradesh State Office
H.No: 10-3-311/13B, MCH No. 818
Road No. 2, Castle Hills Vijay Nagar Colony
Hyderabad - 500 057
Telefax- 040- 2353 4151

CHAIRPERSON'S MESSAGE

Our visionary former President, Dr. A.P. J. Abdul Kalam shared his vision for the future of India through his insightful book, 'Ignited Minds', in which he lucidly describes the potential of an ignited and empowered mind. This book on the common birds and mammals is a similar sincere effort of WWF to ignite young minds to look at nature with a fresh perspective and create an environment of compassion and goodwill towards nature and our fellow creatures. This shift in perspective will eventually help us arrest the destruction and restore the glory of our natural environment.

To discover and recognize your first wild flower, bird or animal is a special feeling- as special as an infant's first step or first word. This marks the beginning of a fascinating new journey of discovery for every naturalist. Every human being is born a naturalist. Seldom has any child eaten a morsel of food without being shown a flower, bird or butterfly. This book on the common birds and mammals of Andhra Pradesh has been written with the intention of educating and stimulating interest about wilderness and diverse life forms, and to motivate amateur nature enthusiasts to become passionate conservationists. It is also for those who love to travel, learn about heritage and different cultures. The book offers an opportunity to the tourist to learn about the natural wealth of the places he visits. This book is not intended to just occupy the shelves of school libraries, but to be used by children and people with an interest in nature to acquaint themselves with the rich natural heritage of Andhra Pradesh

The need for sharing the knowledge about our natural wealth is greater now than ever before, for worldwide we are losing thousands of species every year even before they have been identified, classified and their ecological role determined. This implies that we will be forever unaware of certain ecosystems and the consequences of their collapse on humans, and will be unprepared to respond appropriately. I sincerely hope that this field guide will inspire our younger generation and mobilize them into taking action to conserve our fragile wilderness.

This is the first book of this series on the wildlife heritage of Andhra Pradesh and we aspire to publish other books on nature.

Anil Kumar V. Epur
Chairman
Andhra Pradesh State Committee

WWF for a living planet ®

WWF-INDIA
Andhra Pradesh State Office
H.No: 10-3-311/13B, MCH No. 818
Road No. 2, Castle Hills Vijay Nagar Colony
Hyderabad - 500 057
Telefax- 040- 2353 4151
apso@wwfindia.net

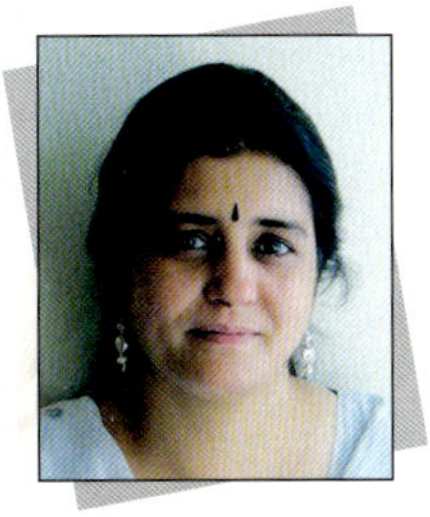

MESSAGE

"Spirit of the forest, spirit of the forest, who seem to melt away, how is it that you do not ask about people? Doesn't a kind of fear grasp you?"- a verse from the later sections of Rig Veda (10.146.1) seem to foresee our present predicament of loss of nature and forest.

We have forgotten the finer nuances and intricate web of life which surrounds us. It is a mad rush from morning to evening when darkness descends not just literally but also metaphorically and we cease to think we do not live alone on this planet. The denizens of the wilderness share this planet with us and today their survival is threatened and they are vanishing at a greater rate than ever since our evolution. Today their survival is threatened by our increasing greed, consumerism and purely materialistic pursuits in an exponential manner.

Their pursuit leaves little time for us to stop and marvel at the wonders of nature and its relation to our own lives. This book is an effort to create an interest amongst all who care and also among those who do not, since...a poor life this is, full of care for ourselves. We have no time to stand and ponder.

FaridaTampal
State Director

R.H. KHWAJA, I.A.S
Chairman & Managing Director

Post Box No. 18, Khairatabad P.O.
Singereni Bhavan, Red Hills,
Hyderabad - 500 004. (A.P)

(A Government Company)

MESSAGE

Andhra Pradesh possesses great diversity- a long coastline, vast scrublands of the Deccan plateau, dense forests in the Eastern Ghats and rich mangroves apart from unique rock formations. This diverse landscape has encouraged species diversity that has been studied by numerous scientists and researchers.

I am delighted to learn that the Andhra Pradesh State Office of WWF has published a guide solely devoted to the common birds and mammals of A.P. I am confident that this publication will provide immense information to all interested students and researchers of nature and biological diversity in the State and will fulfil their long felt need.

We in Singareni Collieries Company Limited (SCCL) have taken some path breaking environmental initiatives since January 2002 for promoting eco-friendly and environmentally sustainable coal mining.We are happy that WWF-India is our partner in this noble effort.

I warmly compliment the Andhra Pradesh State Office of WWF in this timely initiative. I wish the staff of WWF- India, AP State Office further success in their endeavours in promoting the cause of ecological security of the country.

(R.H. KHWAJA)

RACHAMALLU FORGINGS PRIVATE LIMITED
Plot No. 86, CIE Expansion, Gandhinagar, Balanagar,
Hyderabad - 500 037.

MESSAGE

I congratulate WWF- India, APSO for bringing out this lively and colourful book on the birds and animals of Andhra Pradesh. Having visited some of the National Parks and Sanctuaries in our state, it was indeed a pleasure to re-acquaint myself with the birds and mammals described in this field guide. This book will surely find its place among the best books for birdwatchers, naturalists and students.

I wish WWF all success in their efforts for spreading awareness about the rich natural heritage of our state.

R. Sivaprasad Reddy
Managing Director
Rachamallu Forgings Private Limited

V. NAGI REDDY I.A.S.,
Secretary to Government

A.P. Secretariat
Hyderabad - 500 022.

YOUTH ADVANCEMENT TOURISM & CULTURE DEPARTMENT

MESSAGE

Images that come to mind when thinking of Andhra Pradesh are those of ancient temples, rocks, sculptures and culture steeped in deep traditional values. Somewhere amongst thoughts of red-hot pickles and fishermen out to sea, are pictures of lush green rolling hills, waterfalls and open grasslands. This is the heart of Andhra Pradesh.

The book on the common birds and mammals of Andhra Pradesh published by WWF-APSO is a book that would make any nature lover feel at home in this state of glorious natural beauty. WWF has been a forerunner in providing environmental education in Andhra Pradesh. Their effort has also been directed towards promoting eco- tourism, the one area of tourism that the State Government is making huge efforts to develop.

It has always been a pleasure to interact with the representatives of WWF- India, and I wish them all the best with this latest publication. This easy- to- read, superbly coloured field guide at such an affordable price would surely be a welcome addition to school libraries, and the private collection of many-a-naturalists and tourists.

(Secretary to Government)

T. CHATTERJEE, I.A.S.,
Principal Secretary to Government

Environment Forests, Science &
Technology Department
A.P. Secretariat
Hyderabad - 500 022.

MESSAGE

Andhra Pradesh is endowed with extensive and biologically diverse forests. A number of wild birds and mammals inhabit these forests and wetlands. Rare and endangered birds like Jerdon's Courser, Great Indian Bustard, Forest Spotted Owlet (Blewit's) and Yellow Sparrow are found in Andhra Pradesh. Slender Loris, Tiger and Wolf are some rare mammals of the state.Though, of late, there are a few books on common birds of Andhra Pradesh, there is no publication on the mammals of Andhra Pradesh as yet.

The A.P. State Office of WWF-India has been in the forefront of promoting nature conservation, education and awareness in the state. Responding to the need for a common guide on birds and mammals of Andhra Pradesh, this simple and comprehensive field guide has been brought out with illustrations and apt descriptions. I am sure this book will be very useful to children and curious adults and I congratulate WWF-India, Andhra Pradesh State Office for bringing out this excellent publication.

T. CHATTERJEE,
Principal Secretary to Government

S.K. DAS, IFS
Principal Chief Conservator of Forests

Tuljaguda Complex, APHB Buildings,
M.J. Market, D. No. 4-1-714 to 725/1,
Hyderabad-500 001, A.P. (India)
Telephone : 040-24745588 (Off)
040-23390258 (Res)
Fax No. : 040-24745656
e-mail:pccfap@rediff.com

MESSAGE

It is a pleasure to see a field guide appear in the market that concentrates on the fauna of Andhra Pradesh. I am always a believer that the forests of our state and their inhabitant species are very diverse and very much worthy of conservation.

Like WWF, the Forest Department has also been making every effort to bring awareness about the biodiversity of the state through its programmes.

This book by WWF will definitely bring forth a higher level of awareness among the youth of today about the rich natural heritage of the State and motivate them to strive to reach the goal of conserving our biodiversity.

SK DAS
Principal Chief Conservator of Forests

K.S. RAO, IFS
Principal Chief Conservator of Forests (WL)
& Chief Wildlife Warden

Tuljaguda Complex, APHB Buildings,
M.J. Market, D. No. 4-1-714 to 725/1,
Hyderabad-500 001, A.P. (India)
Telephone : 040-24600242 (Off)
040-23411887(Res)
Fax No. : 040-24654755

MESSAGE

Andhra Pradesh is rich in biodiversity and is abundantly gifted to have species like *Pterocarpus santalinus, Cycas beddomei.* The Nagarjunasagar Srisailam Tiger Reserve supports a good tiger population. Rollapadu and Sri Lankamalleshwara Sanctuaries protect the Great Indian Bustard and the Jerdon's Courser respectively. These are perhaps the most important and endangered birds whose habitats need conservation.

Protecting the existing forests, habitats and improving the forest cover outside the Reserve Forests through people's participation has been the task of the Forest Department and it has succeeded in increasing the forest cover by more than 9,000 sq km (Forest Survey of India Report, 2003) during the last few years.

Conserving forests and wildlife is not the task of the Govenment alone, people also have to play an important role. Sensitising our youth and increasing awareness on forests and wildlife is an essental ingredient in protecting our rich biodiversity to pass it on to the coming generations.

WWF India's "The Common Birds and Mammals of Andhra Pradesh" is a sincere effort to educate and motivate people to understand and conserve wildlife. I congratulate the effort of the Andhra Pradesh State Office of WWF-India and look forward to many more publications on biodiversity.

Prl. Chief Conservator of Forests (Wildlife) &
Chief Wildlife Warden

ACKNOWLEDGEMENTS

During a state committee meeting of the AP State Office, the idea of a book on birds and mammals of Andhra Pradesh was floated. A question arose as to who will fund it. This was a big question for an office which was trying to re-orient itself to engage with meaningful conservation activities in the state. The idea immediately found support from all Committee Members including the then Principal Secretary, Youth Advancement, Tourism and Culture, Ms. Chandana Khan, I.A.S. who promised financial assistance. She saw a great opportunity in the book being used as a good field guide for tourists who visit Andhra Pradesh and have an interest in learning about its natural heritage. We thank Ms. Chandana Khan for paving the way for the research work to be started on the book. We also thank Mr. Nagi Reddy, I.A.S. former Secretary of this Department, who gave wholehearted support for the book. We also wish to thank all the staff of the Tourism Department who were very supportive.

Ms. Lakshmi Parthasarathy, I.A.S, Principal Secretary, Youth, Advancement and Tourism Development has always encouraged WWF's activities and we hope to gain from her ideas and her support in her present capacity.

The book was planned in the standard format of most field guides. Timely support from two quarters ensured that we could develop this book with a unique approach. Mr. R.H. Khwaja, I.A.S., previous Chairman and Managing Director of Singareni Collieries Company Limited - a die-hard environmentalist himself - was very enthusiastic and spontaneously promised his support for the book. We place on record our deepest gratitude for his continuous support and encouragement for all our activities. Mr. Narsing Rao, I.A.S., present Chairman and Managing Director of Singareni Collieries Company Limited has been equally helpful and we look forward to a strengthening of bonds between WWF and SCCL under his leadership.

Mr. R.S. Reddy, Managing Director Rachamallu Forgings (P) Ltd., and an avid wildlifer was very excited on being told of the book and issued a cheque on the spot. We thank him for his generosity.

The paper for this wonderful book with its vibrant illustrations and vivid text was donated by Ballarpur Industries Limited (BILT). We thank Mr. Gautam Thapar, Chairman and Managing Director of BILT for his generous donation.

Mr. S.K. Das, I.F.S., PCCF, Mr. Hitesh Malhotra, I.F.S., PCCF (Wildlife) and CWW, Mr. K.S. Rao, I.F.S., former PCCF (Wildlife) and CWW, and Mr. A.V. Joseph, I.F.S., Addl. PCCF from the A.P. Forest Department lent their wholehearted support to our initiative. We thank them for their constant guidance and encouragement.

We are also grateful to Mr. Aasheesh Pittie, Committee Member of WWF A.P. State Committee and former Secretary of Birdwatchers' Society of Andhra Pradesh (BSAP) for contributing to the bird descriptions and going through the illustrations at every stage of their preparation.

The birds and mammals have been illustrated by Mr. Sachin Jaltare. He and his colleague Mr. Anwar Hussain have assiduously designed the book.

We thank the members of the A.P. State Committee for their unstinted support and encouragement.This book took all of three years for publication from the day it was conceived. During this period many young staff and volunteers came into APSO, each of whom added to this book, giving it the shape it has taken today. Ms Archana Waran, Project cum Administration Oficer, Mr. Vikram Aditya, Research Associate and interns Ms. Yashaswini Kumar and Mr. Camaron deserve special mention for putting in dedicated effort to improve the content of this book.

We would like to thank Ms. Aruna Murthy, former Education Officer, for methodically maintaining data files, and Ms. Anuradha Vinod who compiled the chapters on ecosystems and protected areas. Dr. G. Poyyamoli, Reader, Salim Ali School of Ecology and Environmental Sciences, Pondicherry University and Dr. Vasudev Rao of ANGRAU made sure the chapter on Ecosytems was lucid and interesting for the readers. Mr. Sarvottam Rao, I.F.S. (Retd.) and Mr. Ashok Kumar, I.A.S. (Retd.) gave insights on wildlife present in our state's protected areas that could only come from personal experience. Mr. Asad Rahmani, Director of Bombay Natural History Society gave permission for the one-time use of some illustrations from the Book of Indian Birds. Mr. K.S.Rao, I.F.S., PCCF (Wildlife) and CWW permitted the use of the Andhra Pradesh's Protected Areas map. We are thankful to them.

We take this opportunity to thank Mr. Jamshyd Godrej, President, WWF-India and Mr. Ravi Singh, Secretary General and CEO, WWF-India, who have always encouraged and motivated us to pursue excellence in our endeavours.

We are also indebted to the late Ms. Chandini Rao and Mr. Madhu Reddy of Universities Press for their active interest in our book. Their advice in the preparatory stages and supervision during the publication benefited the book greatly.

Our heartfelt gratitude to those who have not been named here, but their contribution, moral support and encouragement remain immense. We thank one and all.

A BRIEF NOTE ON WWF

Birds, mammals and all forms of wildlife have been the prime concern of WWF (World Wide Fund for Nature) since its inception in 1962. In its over forty years of existence, WWF has been attempting to protect wildlife and nature through its conservation initiatives and environmental awareness programmes, not just in India but in more than 90 countries world wide. Among the most noteworthy of its activities are the Eco-regions and the Global Conservation Programmes.

Working in India as a charitable trust since 1969, WWF has done considerable pioneering work to save species such as the Great Indian Bustard. It has been working with the Government to protect tigers through the Project Tiger and prevent wildlife trade through a very successful programme called TRAFFIC, which assists enforcement agencies to investigate, raid and seize wildlife trophies. There have also been projects relating to the Asiatic Lion, the highly endangered Himalayan Newt, the Red Panda, the Mountain Quail, pheasants and several other species. Today, WWF-India is not only the country's largest non government body in the field of conservation, it has also grown into a countrywide network. It has taken on diverse activities in the field of nature protection - ranging from education and capacity building, to field projects in biodiversity, enviro-legal action, policy studies and advocacy, and areas such as religious teachings about conservation.

We believe that conservation begins at home, and the first step is to spread awareness. It is necessary to appreciate the beauty and intricacies of nature and to understand how indispensable the natural world is to us. Without nature, with its myriad creatures, from microscopic bacteria to gigantic trees, our existence on the Earth would be impossible. WWF-India in Andhra Pradesh has been forming Nature Clubs of India (NCIs) in schools and giving an opportunity to students to discover the wilderness around them, motivating them to take action to protect what is rightfully theirs—fresh air, clean water bodies and all natural resources.

INTRODUCTION

" Wildlife?... I wonder sometimes what these animals and birds think of man and how they would describe him if they had the capacity to do so...In spite of our culture and civilisation in many ways, man continues to be not only wild but more dangerous than any of the so-called wild animals... we must try to preserve whatever is left of our forests and the wildlife that inhabit them."

Jawaharlal Nehru

From the foreword to E.P.Gee's "Wildlife of India",1960.

What Pandit Jawaharlal Nehru said four decades ago rings truer today more than ever before. Our country is a land of plenty - having an area of 3. 27 million sq km , where every possible kind of ecosystem, deep rivers, rich mineral reserves, high mountains, thick forests and vast deserts are represented. At times this large canvas overwhelms us making it difficult to perceive Nature's intricacies. Hence, let us take up one state among the 28 and 7 union territories in India, and study what we commonly find here.

Our State

Andhra Pradesh is a land of vast geographic diversity—the arid Deccan Plateau, the broken range of the Eastern Ghats and Nallamalai Hills, seashores along the Bay of Bengal and the mighty Godavari and Krishna rivers create habitats suitable for a wide range of flora and fauna. The state is well endowed with species diversity including one relic species and a few endemic plant species like *Cycas beddomei* and red sanders (*Pterocarpus santalinus*) and animal species like the golden gecko (*Calodactylodes aureus)* and Jerdon's courser (*Rhinoptilus bitorquatus*). Even the shy and elusive slender loris (*Loris tardigradus*) is found in the districts of Kadapa and Chittoor.

Yet, the knowledge of these rare creatures and their more commonly occuring relatives is shared by very few people. In spite of being home to such special species, Andhra Pradesh does not rank very high as a priority area for conservation in India being grossly overshadowed by the internationally recognized and deeply studied biodiversity hotspots, the Eastern Himalayas and Western Ghats. The presence of these hotspots does not by any means lessen the conservational importance of Andhra Pradesh. Before we attempt the herculean task of conservation, let us spare a few moments and familiarize ourselves with the more commonly found fauna of Andhra Pradesh.

How to use this book

This field guide will introduce you to the commonly found birds and mammals of Andhra Pradesh, many of which you might already be familiar with, and some whose existence was unknown to you before now. The use of this book surpasses the political boundaries of the state. In fact, the birds and mammals depicted in this book are also distributed in other parts of the Indian subcontinent. It must be made clear at this point that you might come across species of birds and mammals that do not find a mention in this book . This neither lessens their conservation importance, nor does it necessarily mean that you have discovered a species new to humankind. In this book we have simply attempted to put forth a representation of what is common to Andhra Pradesh.

This book goes beyond merely describing the 180 odd birds and 60 odd common mammals of Andhra Pradesh. It also describes in detail the ecosystems present in our state, their geographic locations and faunal diversity, giving our readers a chance to experience varying landscapes and their inhabitants.

The species described in this book have been arranged according to the widely accepted classification. We have also put together charts for understanding how birds and mammals are classified. This classification will be of interest to biologists. Descriptions are placed adjacent to the images and follow the same sequence as the classification. The birds are described by their physical characters, their habits and breeding behaviour. Mammals are also described in much the same way. The size and vernacular names of mammals also find mention in the book. The section on common mammals draws deeply from 'Book of Indian Animals' by S.H. Prater. The birds are arranged as per the BUCEROS Envis Newsletter for avian ecology.

As you browse through the book, you might notice that the artist has taken special care to illustrate habitats in the backdrop of the animal so as to give a clue to the habitat preference of the creatures. For example, doves are shown sitting deep among thick leaves, while shrikes are seated on leafless branches.

Wherever possible, we have tried to show animal sizes proportionate to each other on the same page. This was not possible in certain cases where the animals had a vast size difference and showing them proportionately would mean compromising on the clarity and details of the illustration. A handy index at the end will help readers navigate through the book. Both common and scientific names are listed in it.

As you discover more and more about the species diversity of A.P., you are bound to get curious about places you might see them in. Hence we have dedicated an entire chapter on the National Parks and Wildlife Sanctuaries in Andhra Pradesh. Each protected area has a note on how to reach there, when to visit, whom to contact and what wildlife could be sighted. This chapter will assist you in your exploration of wilderness areas of the State and gain memorable experiences in the field.

We have not treated this book as simply another field guide; one of the purposes of the book is to draw young readers towards meaningful conservation. If you have an interest in getting involved with wildlife research or conservation, you will find our list of local and national wildlife NGOs helpful.

We have dedicated an entire chapter on Scheduled animals. This chapter describes the provisions in the Indian Wildlife (Protection) Amendment Act, 2002, No. 1 of 2003 and the IUCN Red List. The purpose of the Act and the reason for placing flora and fauna in particular schedules is also explained. This chapter can make a handy reference for understanding the value of a certain bird or animal and the dynamics of its relationship with humans. Though we have quite a few species in the state that are rare enough to find mention in these listings, we have described the status of only those common birds and mammals that have been described in the book. Nevertheless, you might find this chapter useful for reporting wildlife related crimes or conservation efforts you may have witnessed.

MAP DEPICTING
PROTECTED AREAS OF ANDHRA PRADESH

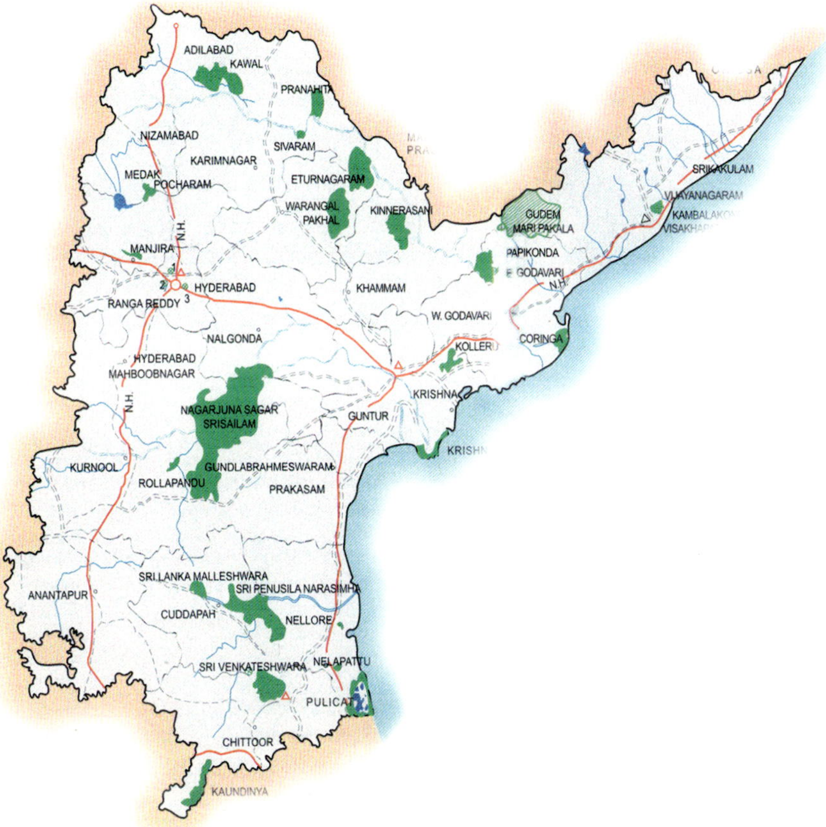

ECOSYSTEMS IN ANDHRA PRADESH

When a community of plants and animals lives together in a certain area that is defined by a set of climatic conditions, it operates in synchronicity with the environment, and the system thus formed is an Ecosystem. Within a large ecosystem, each organism occupies a special niche, or place for itself where it lives, feeds and breeds. This is its habitat. For example, a bulbul's habitat may be a clump of *Lantana* bushes, while it belongs to a scrub forest ecosystem. A fiddler crab's habitat is a mangrove ecosystem where it lives, feeds and propagates. Ecosystems may be of various sizes. A pond, a tract of forest or a scrub jungle would also be ecosystems, since they have their own characteristic organisms and processes.

Andhra Pradesh ranks high in terms of natural resources as a virtue of its geographical characteristics and varied landscapes. By area, it is the fifth largest in the country, being located towards the centre of the Indian peninsula. It has the second longest coastline among Indian states, which stretches 974 km along the Bay of Bengal. The Deccan Plateau extends along the North and West of the state, gently sloping eastwards till it encounters the Eastern Ghats. The Eastern Ghats are a long broken chain of hills running parallel to the eastern seacoast of India, although they are largely absent in the alluvial delta region between the Godavari and Krishna rivers where numerous tributaries merge with each of these mighty rivers. The Eastern Ghats constitute a number of smaller hill ranges such as the Papikonda hills, Nallamalai hills, Velikonda hills, Seshachalam hills, etc. Beyond the Ghats lie the fertile coastal plains. These four regions provide four biotic provinces. The largest is the Deccan Plateau covering 53% of the land area, followed by the Central Plateau covering 35%, and the Eastern Ghats and Coastal Plains covering 12% together.

Summers in Andhra Pradesh are hot and dry with temperatures shooting up to 46°C, while winter temperatures seldom fall below 8° Celsius. This variation in topography and climate supports a variety of ecotypes, flora and fauna. Three major river systems Krishna, Godavari and Pennar irrigate the lands as they flow eastward to meet the Bay of Bengal. Mangrove forests flourish along the estuaries where the three rivers meet the sea. Pulicat Lake, one of the longest lagoons in South Asia, is also located in this state. This lake is a haven for a variety of resident and migratory birds.

With such a wide range of geographic and climatic conditions, it is but natural for the state to have a diverse range of forests. Five major forest types - tropical dry deciduous, southern tropical dry deciduous, southern tropical thorn forests, littoral forests and tidal swamp mangrove forests are represented in the state. There are also grasslands, riverine forests and brackish water lagoons that add to the rich ecological diversity of Andhra Pradesh.

Marine Ecosystem:

Most scientists hypothesize that all life on earth originated in the sea. Open seas hold 10 per cent of all oceanic life forms. They have unique food chains, relationships and processes that make them function as a marine ecosystem. It is estimated that about 150 million people in the world rely on fisheries, aquaculture, and associated activities.

Marine life-forms, especially fish, shrimps and molluscs, are of economic importance to us. Andhra Pradesh contributes to nearly 40 per cent of the total marine product exports from the country. The sector is providing direct and indirect employment to over 14 lakh people particularly in the rural sector. There are 508 fishing villages along the coast.

The state has a long coastline of 974 km bordering the Bay of Bengal to its east. Dolphins, whales, turtles, fish and many sea faring birds are the more commonly sighted wildlife in the open seas.

Inter-tidal Zone Ecosystem:

The coastal zone of the ocean is typically a shallow water zone with a depth of less than 200 metres. This zone also varies as per geographic conditions of the adjoining coasts. There may be estuaries, mangroves or coral reefs along the coasts, each having a unique ecosystem in place.

The organisms living in inter-tidal zones are extremely hardy. They have adapted to the rough conditions of the shoreline where temperature and salinity change with every tide. They are covered by water for some part of the day and are exposed to sunlight for the rest of the day. The best-adapted organisms can live high up on the shore, exploiting a rich but difficult environment. This zone is usually rocky, with nooks and crannies ideal for many species of molluscs like limpets, top-shells, winkles which graze on the algae and the seaweeds growing on the shore. These, in turn, are the food for crabs, fish and other molluscs. Higher birds like oystercatchers, gulls, terns etc again feed on the crabs, fishes and other molluscs.

Inter-tidal zones are seen at the sandy beaches of Visakhapatnam, Machilipatnam Coringa's mangroves and in the estuarine Pulicat lake.

Mangrove Ecosystem:

Mangrove is a generic term that describes a cluster of species belonging to different families with different adaptations for essentially one function, tolerating high salinity. Mangrove forests form a peculiar habitat as they grow on the boundary of land and sea and need varying amounts of saline and freshwater to survive. The world over, mangroves are found only between 30° N and 30° S latitudes and are extensions of the tropical rain forests towards the sea. India has around 70 species of mangroves.

Mangrove forest flora is extremely hardy, capable of surviving strong currents, tidal forces, strong winds, soil and water salinity, poor soil and slushy grounds.

Stilt roots for additional support, pneumatophores (air breathing roots), salt glands on the trunk to excrete excess salt, leathery leaves and vivipary (young saplings grow on the parent tree until they are big enough to avoid complete submersion during high tide) are the special adaptations that give mangrove trees the capacity to withstand tough inter-tidal conditions.

Mangroves provide an ideal home for many animals including shrimps, fish fingerlings, crocodiles, tigers, deer and birds. The fishing cat, an exceptionally adapted beautiful feline, is another representative of the mangrove ecosystem.

In Andhra Pradesh mangrove forests occur in Coringa near Kakinada in the estuaries of the Godavari River, Machilipatnam and Nizampatnam along the estuary of the Krishna River and in smaller patches along smaller channels and inlets along the coast.

Estuarine Ecosystem:

An estuarine ecosystem is a rich and fertile ecosystem that is almost as productive as coral reefs. Estuaries are fed by silt, mud, remains of plants and other organic material brought down by the rivers which mixes with the nutrient-rich material that flows in with the tides. Though the water is muddy and does not aid in photosynthesis, the water itself provides a rich supply of food. Oligohaline (i.e. slightly salty) waters are the best areas for fishes to breed and thrive. Godavari and Krishna river deltas are good examples of estuarine ecosystems.

Freshwater Ecosystem:

Rivers, streams, lakes and wetlands are sources of fresh water for terrestrial life forms. Rivers and streams form when runoff and groundwater collect in low-lying channels, to run down slopes and fall into oceans or lakes. Water accumulates in large depressions through precipitation, runoff, stream flow and groundwater flows to make lakes. Some lakes are manmade, built to serve the community. These are generally referred to as reservoirs. Depending on nutrient content, fresh water bodies may be eutrophic, mesotrophic or oligotrophic. Eutrophic lakes are rich in nutrients like nitrogen and phosphorous and support large populations of plankton. They have poor fish diversity. Oligotrophic lakes have crystal clear water, are poor in nutrients and therefore low in biotic productivity. Plants like *Eichorrnia* thrive in nutrient rich waters of eutrophied lakes, and are indicators of a lake's nutrient status. Mesotrophic lakes have water lilies, lotuses and even algae. Herbivores like the Sambar enjoy feeding in these waters.

Freshwater wetlands remain partially submerged by fresh water through most of the year. Wetlands include habitats like marshes, swamps, backwaters of reservoirs and ponds. Wetlands are highly productive environments with more plants and fish, birds and animals than in terrestrial habitats. They function as 'ecotones', transition zones between different habitats that have characteristics of both aquatic and terrestrial ecosystems.

Wetlands have often been described as the kidneys of the landscape because they filter out sediment and pollution from the surrounding environment and discharge cleaner water to rivers and lakes. In this manner, wetlands act as both sink and source, storing and passing on vital resources to their local environment. Kolleru Lake, a natural balancing lake between the deltas of Krishna and Godavari rivers and Pulicat Lake in Nellore District are the most important wetlands of Andhra Pradesh. Warangal, Prakasam, Visakhapatnam, Nizamabad, Nellore, Guntur, Cudappah, Anantapur and Adilabad also have important wetlands.

Grassland Ecosystem:

World over, grasslands are being converted into agricultural lands, pushing the resident wildlife towards the brink of extinction. The Great Indian Bustard of Rollapadu Sanctuary in Kurnool District is an example of this. There were over 60 Great Indian Bustards in the sanctuary in 1985, but their number has dwindled to an estimated 15- 20 in 2001. Grasslands in Andhra Pradesh are characterised by open grassy plains and dry, thorny bushes. Various kinds of animals, birds and reptiles such as scorpions, Russell's Viper, Indian Cobra, Great Indian Bustard, Indian Roller, Sparrow, Myna, Black Buck, Common Mongoose, Wild Boar, Jungle Cat, Jackal, Wolf and Indian Fox inhabit these grasslands.

Thorn Forest Ecosystem:

Tropical thorn forests occur where the weather is hot and dry for around seven months in a year. There is little rain in thorn forests, usually averaging 250 to 500 millimetres a year (about 10 to 20 inches). During the monsoon the forest looks lush green. The trees here do not grow beyond 10 meters, and are characteristically thorny and frequently stem succulent. Once the monsoon is over and dry weather returns, trees shed their leaves and the ground is bare except for a few tufted plants in bunches. Grasses are uncommon. Forest fires often break out in peak summers. Thorn forests usually grow in areas with black soil.

Sri Lankamalleswara Sanctuary, Kadapa district harbours mixed thorn forests along with dry deciduous forests. This beautiful sanctuary is home to red sanders trees, endemic to this region and *Carissa caranda* bushes that form a major flora of the forest. Jerdon's courser, one of the most endangered bird species in the world is reported from this Sanctuary. Southern thorn forests are present in Kaundinya Wildlife Sanctuary of Chittoor District, the only place in Andhra Pradesh where elephants can be seen in the wild.

The Deccan Plateau south division of Andhra Pradesh is an important dry and thorny scrub dominated by *Albizzia, Harwickia* and *Acacia* trees. This is a corridor for elephant movement from protected areas of the Western Ghats to the forests of the Eastern Ghats.

Dry Deciduous Forest Ecosystem:

Dry deciduous forests occur where there is an average rainfall of 800-1000 mm per year, falling mostly in one season. Broad leaved deciduous trees shed their leaves in the dry season to prevent excessive water loss. A few patches of evergreen trees, short grasses and shrubs also grow in this ecosystem. On the advent of monsoon, the entire forest wears a gown of green. The forest floor is covered with moss and fungi during the wet season. The trees produce a variety of fruits, seeds and berries that are dispersed by animals, birds and the wind. Deciduous trees have delicate, flattened leaves to catch sunlight. They grow slower than conifers as they shed their leaves in winter or sometimes even in summer . The soil is very fertile. In fact, some of the great agricultural regions are found in this biome. For this reason very few original deciduous forests exist in the world today.

Nagarjunsagar Srisailam Tiger Reserve in Andhra Pradesh is a fine example of dry deciduous forests in the state. Kawal and Pranahita Wildlife Sanctuaries also have dry deciduous forests with bamboo, *Terminalia* and *Pterocarpus* as the key floral species. Eturnagaram Sanctuary in Warangal, Papikonda Wildlife Sanctuary in East Godavari and Kinnerasani Sanctuary in Khammam also harbour dry deciduous teak forests.

Evergreen Forest Ecosystem:

Trees in an evergreen forest do not shed their leaves all at once. Therefore, the forest looks green throughout the year. The forest floor is covered with dense vegetation. Trees here compete with each other for sunlight and are very tall. One can find a variety of ferns, mosses and fungi in this ecosystem.

The Eastern Highlands of the Deccan Plateau, which covers the states of Andhra Pradesh and Madhya Pradesh, has some rich tropical evergreen and semi evergreen forests. This includes the northern parts of the Eastern Ghats and several associated hill ranges.

Sri Venkateshwara Wildlife Sanctuary nestled in the picturesque Seshachalam hills in Chittoor District also has Evergreen forests.This forest is home to the golden gecko, slender loris and *Cycas beddomeii* , all three of which are endemic to this region. Gundlabrahmeswaram Wildlife Sanctuary, a part of the Nallamalai hill range is another evergreen forest where one can see giant squirrels.

NATIONAL PARKS AND WILDLIFE SANCTUARIES OF ANDHRA PRADESH

Andhra Pradesh has four National Parks, twenty-two Wildlife Sanctuaries, thirteen Deer Parks and three Zoological Parks. The total protected area is 12,903.32 sq. km.

The mangrove forests in Andhra Pradesh cover an area of 333 sq km. Wetlands and water bodies cover 2950 sqkm and rivers cover an area of 817 sqkm.

National Parks of Andhra Pradesh

Kasu Brahmananda Reddy National Park, Hyderabad (1.425 sq.km)

Named after the late former Chief Minister of Andhra Pradesh, this National Park is located in the heart of the city. Its strategic location acts as the green lungs of the city and the beautiful flora and fauna abound in it. The park is steep on the northern side with a gentle slope and rocky outcrops on the southern side. The geology of the park conforms to the typical Deccan Plateau type.

Forest Type: A typical grassland locally called 'Rawand'. It has components of southern tropical dry deciduous forest in the Archaean Gneissic region containing the last vestigial representatives of the endemic flora of Hyderabad region.

Flora: The park is home to over 600 species of plants viz. *Acacia* species, Crab's eye Creeper, Teak, Sandalwood, Neem, Flame of the Forest, Axle Wood, East Indian Walnut, *Diospyros chloroxylon*, Coromandel Ebony, Jujub and *Ficus* species.

Fauna: Jungle Cat, Small Indian Civet, Wild Boar, Common Mongoose, 130 species of birds, 30 species of reptiles including the Indian rock python and 30 species of butterflies. A large number of peacocks can be found roaming freely.

Best Season to Visit: All year around.

Accessibility : Jubilee Hills is located in the heart of Hyderabad.

Contact : Divisional Forest Officer, Wildlife Management, Hyderabad. (Ph: 040-23607663) or Forest Range Officer, KBR Park (23555463)

Mahavir Harini Vanasthalipuram National Park, Hyderabad (14.95 sq km)

Located on the Hyderabad-Vijayawada Highway, this National Park is home to the beautiful Black Buck, the State Animal of Andhra Pradesh.

Forest type: The forest type is dry deciduous with scrub jungle and gently rolling grasslands.

Flora : Sandalwood, Ghost tree, Indian Kino, Flame of the Forest, Teak, Indian Laburnum, Rosewood, etc.

Fauna: Civet, Porcupine, Wild Boar, Black Buck, Chital and 30 species of reptiles and over 120 species of birds.

Best Season to Visit: All year round.

Accessibility : Vanasthalipuram, 15 km by road from Hyderabad on the Hyderabad-Vijaywada highway NH-9.

Contact : DFO, WLM, Hyderabad (Ph : 040-23607663, 9440810629) or FRO, MHV NP (Ph : 040-25502180, 9440810583).

Mrugavani National Park, Chilkur, Hyderabad (3.60 sq.km)

This National Park is located on the outskirts of Hyderabad, in Ranga Reddy district. It is nestled between two reservoirs, Osmansagar and Himayatsagar. This is an urban forest ecosystem with grasslands supporting a mixed fauna.

Forest type: Southern tropical dry deciduous forest containing the last vestiges of Hyderabad endemic flora.

Flora: Bamboo, Teak, Sandalwood, Flame of the Forest, Indian Laburnum etc.

Fauna: Leopard, Jungle Cat, Civet Cat, Mongoose, Wild Boar, Sambar, Chital, Monitor Lizard, Indian Rock Python, Russell's Viper, Spectacled Cobra, various species of birds and butterflies.

Best Season to Visit: All year round.

Accessibility : 25 km from Hyderabad.

Contact : DFO, Hyderabad (Ph : 040-23607663, 9440810161) or FRO, Mrugavani National Park, Chilkur (Ph : 923235135, 9440810582).

Sri Venkateshwara National Park, Tirupati (525.97 sq km)

Nestling in sylvan Seshachalam and Tirumala hills, Sri Venkateshwara National Park is located in Chitoor and Kadapa districts. This beautiful national park covers the Rajampet and Chitoor East forest divisions of Andhra Pradesh.

Forest Type: The park has a dry deciduous mixed forests with patches of moist deciduous forests in the valleys.

Flora: The park houses some rare and endemic plant species like Red Sanders, Indian Olibanum, Flame of the Forest, *Terminalia pallida*, *Syzigium alternifolia*, *Shorea talura, Shorea thumbergiana, Cycas beddomei* (a living fossil), Sandalwood etc. The park has as many as 1,500 species of vascular plants.

Fauna: The forest harbours certain rare and endemic animals like the Slender Loris,

Indian Giant Squirrel, Mouse Deer, Golden Gecko (that was discovered after 100 years). Tiger, Leopard, Wild Dog, Hyena, Jackal, Fox, Civet Cat, Jungle Cat, Sloth Bear, Wild Boar, Sambar, Chital, Chowsingha, Tree Shrew, Flying Lizard and Monitor Lizard are also present here. Over 150 species of birds are found in this park.
Best Season to Visit: All year round.
Accessibility : 10 km from Tirupati by road.
Accomodation: Forest Rest Houses at Tirupati, Rajampet, Talakona and Bakarpet.
Contact : Conservator of Forests (WLM), Tirupati (Ph: 0877- 2231887) or Divisional Forest Officer, (WLM), Sri Vekateswara NP, Tirupati (Ph. 0877-2280980, 9440810303).

Wildlife Sanctuaries of Andhra Pradesh

Coringa Wildlife Sanctuary (235.70 sq km), East Godavari District

Coringa wildlife sanctuary is the largest surviving patch of mangrove forests in the State with more than 65 mangrove tree species. Coringa is located in the estuary of River Godavari where it enters the Bay of Bengal in East Godavari District. It is home to the rare, endangered Smooth Indian Otter, Fishing Cat and the Estuarine Crocodile.
Forest type: The mangrove tidal swamps located in the Godavari estuary are one of the oldest formations of mangrove ecosystems.
Flora: There are 24 species of mangroves belonging to 19 genera and 15 families dominated by *Avicennia marina* (Tellamada) and *Avicennia officinalis* (Nallamada). *Schyphyphora hydrophyllaces* (Narathanduga) is an endemic species. Rare species like *Sonneratia alba* (Pedda Kalinga) , *Rhizophora mucronata* (Uppu Ponna), *Tamarix troupii* (Palivelu) are also found here.
Fauna: 180 species of fish, 20 species of molluscs, 40 species of crustaceans. It provides a fine habitat for Grey Herons, Egrets, Spotbilled Pelicans, Painted Storks and is home to the Smooth Coated Indian Otter and the Fishing Cat. A variety of reptiles including marine turtles and estuarine crocodiles are also found here. An 18 km long sand pit in the North Eastern side is a nesting spot for Olive Ridley turtles.
Best Season to Visit: October to June
Accessibility : 20 km from Kakinada Railway station and 70 km from Rajahmundry by bus.
Accomodation: Forest Rest Houses at Coringa, Kakinada and Rajahmundry.
Contact : DFO (WLM), Rajahmundry, East Godavari District (Ph. 0883-2478643, 9440810044) or Forest Range Officer, Kakinada (Ph: 0884-2367460, 9440810238, 9440810235).

Eturnagaram Wildlife Sanctuary (806 sq km), Warangal District

The Eturnagaram Wildlife Sanctuary is situated in the Warangal district of Andhra Pradesh on the banks of river Godavari along the border of Andhra Pradesh and Chattisgarh States. The dense forest is home to the largest Gaur populations in the state.

Forest type: Dry deciduous mixed teak forest and riverine forest. Undulating country with low hills.

Flora: The forest contains mainly teak with Bamboo, *Pterocarpus, Anogeissus, Buchanania,Terminalia tomentosa,* Arjun, Axle Wood, Cudappah Almond, Kino etc.

Fauna: The park has superb faunal diversity with carnivores like Tiger, Leopard, Wolf, Wild Dog, Jackal, Fox, Jungle Cat and Sloth Bear. Wild Boar, Gaur, Sambhar, Chital, Nilgai, Barking Deer, Four Horned Antelope are the herbivores in this forest. Other unique mammals such as Giant Squirrel and Tree Shrew are present. Snakes like the Common Krait, Indian Rock Python and several species of birds are also present here.

Accessibility: 90 km from Warangal / Kazipet (Railway station), 250 km. from Hyderabad by road.

Best Season to Visit: October to May

Accommodation: Cottages and Rest House at Tadvai. Forest Rest House, Hanumakonda at Warangal and ITDA Guest House at Eturnagaram.

Contact: Divisional Forest Officer, (WLM), Warangal. (Ph: 0870-2431546, 9440810095) or Forest Range Officer, Eturnagaram (Ph: 08717-231240)

Gundla Bramheshwaram Wildlife Sanctuary (1194 sq km), Kurnool and Prakasam districts

This is the best surviving typical Nallamalai forest with pristine forests rich in ethno-botanical value. The perennial Gundla Kamma River meanders through the eastern part of the sanctuary.

Forest type: Dry deciduous mixed teak and the last surviving in Nallamalai range. Rich in plant life with scenic forest areas.

Flora: Teak, Kino, *Terminalia tomentosa*, Arjun, Axle Wood, Rosewood, Jungle Cork Tree, Indian Olibanum, Bamboo.

Fauna: Tiger, Panther, Wild Dog, Jungle Cat, Sloth bear, Hanuman Langur, Bonnet Macaque, Indian Pangolin, Sambar, Nilgai, Chital, Chowsingha, Mouse deer, Giant Squirrel, Indian Rock Python, Spectacled Cobra, Marsh Crocodile.

Best Season to Visit: October to May.

Accessibility: 30 kilometers from Nandyal Railway Station. 100km from Kurnool.

Accomodation: Inspection bungalow at Nandyal (Kurnool Distt), Forest Rest House at Diguvamitta (Prakasam Distt).

Contact: District Forest Officer, Nandyal (Ph:08514-242463, 9440810059) or Forest Range Officer, GBM Range, (Ph: 08514-245785), D.F.O. Nandyal (Ph : 08514-242463).

Koundinya Wildlife Sanctuary (357.60 sq. km.), Chittoor District

Kaundinya sanctuary is the only Elephant Reserve in the entire state. Elephant herds have returned to this area after about 200 years.This sanctuary comes under Project Elephant, in the Palamaner-Kuppam forest ranges of Chittoor district. Horsley Hills, the famous tourist hill station is located in this sanctuary.

Forest type: Southern tropical dry deciduous and thorn forest.

Flora: Bamboo, *Lagerstroemia lanceolata, Ficus* spp, Albizzias and Acacias are found here.

Fauna: Leopard, Jackal, Jungle Cat, Sloth Bear, Indian Elephant, Wild Boar, Sambar, Chital, Chowsingha, Porcupine and Slender Loris. Grey Jungle Fowl and Star Tortoise are also present here.

Best Season to Visit: October to April.

Accessibility: 50 km. by road from Chittoor.

Accomodation: Forest Guest House at Palamner, Madanapalli and APTDC cottages at Horsley Hills.

Contact: Divisional Forest Officer, Chittoor (West) (Ph: 08572-232458, 9440810624) or Forest Range Officer, Palamner (Ph:08579-251027, 9440810454).

Kambalkonda Wildlife Sanctuary (70.70 sq km), Visakhapatnam District

This sanctuary is located in the Kambalkonada Reserve forest, an urban forest close to the city of Visakhapatnam. This has a hilly terrain and steep slopes, excellent for nature trails and treks.

Forest type: Dry evergreen forest mixed with scrub and meadows.

Flora: Teak, Bamboo and low scrub forests.

Fauna: The mammalian fauna is represented by Leopard, Jackal, Wild Dog, Sloth Bear, Wild Boar, Sambhar, Chital and Barking Deer. The reptilian fauna includes Monitor Lizard, Indian Rock Python etc.

Best Season to Visit: Round the year.

Accessibility: 5 km from Vizag, in the outskirts of the city.

Accomodation: APTDC's Guest House, Z.P. Guest House and many lodges in Vizag.

Contact: Divisional Forest Officer, Visakhapatnam (Ph: 0891-2563784, 9440810034, 9440810194)

Kawal Wildlife Sanctuary (893 sq km) , Adilabad District

This pristine forest located in Adilabad district is a tiger sanctuary and was the first sanctuary to be declared in Andhra Pradesh. Kawal has one of the richest teak forests in the State. The river Kadam flows along the western parts of the Sanctuary.

Forest type: Dry deciduous Forest with bamboo brakes.

Flora: Teak, Bamboo, *Terminalia* , *Pterocarpus, Anogeisus, Cassias,* Kino.

Fauna: Kawal has a good carnivore population. Tiger, Leopard, Wolf, Wild Dog (Dhole), Sloth Bear and Jackal. Herbivores like Nilgai, Chinkara, Chital, Sambhar, Chowsingha, Gaur, Mouse Deer and several species of birds and reptiles including Indian Rock Python and Spectacled Cobra.

Best Season to Visit: November to May.

Accessibility: 50 km from Mancherial, 80 km from Nirmal .

Accomodation: Forest Rest Houses at Jannaram and Mancherial. Dormitory for 20 people at Jannaram and I.T.D.C. Rest House at Utnoor.

Contact: Divisional Forest Officer, (WLM) Jannaram, Adilabad Dist. (Ph. 08739-236224, 9440810503) or Forest Range Officer, Jannaram (Ph. 08739-236688, 236224, 9440810427)

Kinnersani Wildlife Sanctuary (635.40 sq km), Khammam District

This sanctuary includes the Kinnerasani Reservoir. There are densely forested islands in the middle of the reservoir.

Forest type: Dry mixed deciduous forest.

Flora: Teak, bamboo, *Terminalia spp* (Maddi), Axle Wood, etc.

Fauna: Tiger, Leopard, Hyena, Jackal, Wild Dog, Sloth Bear, Wild Boar, Sambar, Chital, Chowsingha, Chinkara and several species of birds such as Peafowl, Grey Jungle Fowl, Quail, Francolin, Doves, Ducks, Teals, Spoonbill, Nukta (Comb Duck), Openbill Stork etc. The reservoir harbours Marsh Crocodiles.

Best Season to Visit: October to May.

Accessibility: 15 km from Bhadrachalam Road railway station, 15 km from Kothagudem and 25 km from the temple town of Bhadrachalam.

Accomodation: Forest Rest Houses , Paloncha, Kothagudem and Bhadrachalam. APTDC Guest House at Bhadrachalam(Ph: 08743-234942).

Contact: Divisional Forest Officer, (WLM), Khammam (Ph. 08744-254125, 9440810087), Forest Range Officer, Paloncha (Ph. 9440810349, 9440810344).

Kolleru Wildlife Sanctuary (308. 55 sq km), West Godavari and Krishna Districts

Kolleru Lake is the largest fresh water lake in the state and a notified Ramsar site. It is a freshwater wetland supporting a rich biodiversity. The area notified as a sanctuary covers part of the lake to an extent of 308.55 sq km. But at the highest flood level (+10.71 contour MSL) recorded in 1964 floods, the lake spreads over 954 sq km.

Flora: The macrophytes include the free floating, rooted floating-leaved, emergent and submerged types. Kikkisa reed (*Phragmites karka*), typha grass (*Typha augustata*) and eel grass (*Valisnaria spiralis*) are the dominant species. *Ipomea aquatica* and water hyacinth (*Eichhornia crassipes*), which are weeds, have invaded this lake due to water pollution.

Fauna: 63 species of fish and five species of prawns, the most popular being the Tiger prawn (*Pinnaeus monodon*). 15 species of native fish are either depleted or have disappeared due to large scale fishing and prawn farms set up on the lake bed.

185 bird species have been recorded which includes four rare bird species and 12 endangered ones. A number of birds like Brahminy Ducks, Openbill Storks, Herons, Spotbills, sometimes Flamingoes and Grey Pelicans visit this lake.
Best Season to Visit: October to May.
Accessibility: 2 km from Kaikalur town; 35 km from Eluru town and railway station and 60 km from Vijayawada Railway Station.
Accommodation: Forest Rest House at Vijayawada and Eluru. Private lodges at Kaikalur and Bhimavaram.
Contact: Divisional Forest Officer (WLM), Eluru, West Godavari District. (Ph: 08812-232356, 9440810147) or Forest Range Officer, Eluru. (Ph: 08812-239578).

Krishna Wildlife Sanctuary (194.81 sq km), Krishna and Guntur Districts

The mangrove forest in Krishna Wildlife Sanctuary is the last surviving mangrove forest in Krishna River Estuary with distinct flora and fauna.
Flora: The sanctuary supports rich mangrove floral communities, covering an area of approximately 1292 ha including the area near the light house. *Avicennia marina*, Arjun (*Terminalia arjuna*) and the Blinding Tree are the dominant species. The vegetation is sparse in Sorlagondi, Nachugunta, Lankivanidibba and Yelichetladibba Reserve Forests. *Prosopis* invasion is a serious threat to the mangrove biodiversity.
Fauna: Fishing Cat and Smooth-coated Indian Otter are the common mammals of this sanctuary. Estuarine crocodile, turtles and several species of resident and migratory birds are also present.
Best Season to Visit: October to February.
Accessibility: 25 km from Repalle in Guntur District. 80 km by road from Vijayawada Railway station (Krishna District).
Accomodation: Forest rest houses at Vijayawada and at Repalle, Guntur district.
APTDC's Berm Park at Vijaywada and Surya Lanka Beach Resort in Bapatla are also available.
Contact: Divisional Forest Officer (WLS), Eluru, West Godavari District (Ph: 08812-232356, 9440810147) or Forest Range Officer, Eluru (Ph: 08812-239578).

Manjira Wildlife Sanctuary (20 sq km), Medak District

Located in the Medak district of Andhra Pradesh on river Manjira which is a tributary to River Godavari between Manjira and Singur barrages. The sanctuary has nine small islands, which are major nesting sites for birds. An Environmental Education Centre with a museum, a library, and an auditorium is located here.

Forest type: Riverine habitat.
Flora: Dominated by hydrophytes and weeds such as *Prosopis, Ipomea aquatica,* Babul and reeds are also found.
Fauna: Marsh crocodile, freshwater turtles and a number of water birds such as Herons, Storks, Teals, Ducks, Geese, Moorhens etc. Painted storks nest in this habitat.
Best Season to Visit: October to June.
Accessibility: 5 km from Sangareddy town, 60 km by road from Hyderabad.
Accommodation: Inspection bungalows at Sangareddy, Singur and Sadasivpet. For accommodation contact Executive Engineer, R&B Department, Sangareddy, Medak District.
Contact: Divisional Forest Officer (WLM), Medak (Ph: 08452-222591, 9440810119) or Divisional Forest Officer, Planning and Extension, Sangareddy (Ph: 08452-276317).

Nelapattu Bird Sanctuary (4.58 sq km), Nellore District

Nelapattu bird sanctuary is located in Nellore district of Andhra Pradesh to the north of Pulicat Lake close to the Tamil Nadu state border. Spread over 4.86 sqkm, it is one of the largest Pelicanries in South East Asia, with more than 1,500 Grey Pelicans breeding here every year. The villagers of Nelapattu offer protection and care for the birds. An annual Flamingo Festival is held every year in February.
Forest type: Fresh water tanks with *Barringtonia* trees which provide nesting sites to the birds. Southern dry evergreen scrub forests surround the sanctuary.
Flora: *Barringtonia acutangula*, *Prosopis,* Babul trees and *Ipomoea* reeds are the dominant species here.
Fauna: The avifauna includes around 220 species of birds of which around 60 species are migratory. They are Black Bellied Tern, Tufted Pochard, Spot Billed Pelican, Wigeon, Pied Crested Cuckoo, Asian Openbill Stork, Spoonbills, White Ibis, Cormorant, Indian Shag, Night Heron, Teals and Ducks. Mammals include Jackal, and Chital.
Accessibility: 23 km by road from Sullurpet railway station; 80 km by road from Chennai on Chennai-Kolkata road (N.H.5). Chennai is the nearest airport.
Best season to visit: October to March
Accomodation: Inspection bungalow at Sullurpet; Garden Hotel, 3 km from Sullurpet on NH 5, R.R. Residency, a private lodge.
Contact: Divisional Forest Officer (WLM), Sullurpeta (Ph. 08623-242158, 9440810071).

Pakhal Wildlife Sanctuary (860.20 sq km), Warangal District

This is one of the oldest sanctuaries of Andhra Pradesh. The sanctuary is located on the banks of the Pakhal Lake on a large plateau surrounded by low hills. Pakhal Lake is a manmade lake, excavated by the Kakatiyas in 1213 AD. The sanctuary forms partly the catchment for two drainage systems viz; one draining to Godavari River through Laknavaram tank and the other joining Krishna River through Munneru tributary. It used to be the preferred hunting area for the Nizams and their guests.

Forest type: Dry deciduous mixed forest.

Flora: Teak, Arjun, Bamboo, Mahua, Butter Tree, Maddi, Kino.

Fauna: The Pakhal Lake in the midst of the forest attracts a large number of migratory birds like Ducks, Teals, Storks, Ibises and Cormorants. The reptilian life includes Common Krait, Indian Rock Python, Spectacled Cobra and Marsh Crocodile. Tiger, Leopard, Jackal, Fox, Wild Dog, Hyena, Sloth Bear, Wild Boar, Gaur, Sambar, Chital and Nilgai are the mammals present.

Best Season to visit: November to June.

Accessibility: 60 km from Warangal / Kazipet Rly Stn. 230 km from Hyderabad by road.

Accomodation: Forest Guest House at Warangal. There is an APTDC Guest House near REC in Warangal. There are also many private guest houses at Hanumakonda and Warangal.

Contact: Divisional Forest Officer (WLM), Subedari, Warangal (Ph:0870-2431546) or Forest Range Officer, Eturnagaram (Ph: 08717-231240).

Papikonda Wildlife Sanctuary (591 sqkm), East Godavari

Papikonda Wildlife Sanctuary extends over parts of three districts–East Godavari, West Godavari, Khammam on the East and West banks of Godavari. This sanctuary is situated in the densely forested Papikonda Hill Range of the Eastern Ghats.

Forest type: Dense dry deciduous teak forest, continuous bamboo brakes.

Flora: Teak, Ghost tree, *Terminalia arjuna*, Kino, Gooseberry, *Acacia* spp and Axle wood are the common trees in Papikonda.

Fauna: Mammals include Tiger, Leopard, Jackal, Wild Dog, Hyena, Sloth Bear, Gaur, Sambhar, Chital, Black Buck, Four Horned Antelope and Mouse Deer. The bird fauna includes Hornbill, Brahminy Duck and various teals. Reptiles like Monitor Lizard, Spectacled Cobra, Marsh Crocodile are found here.

Best Season to Visit: October to May.

Accessibility: 50 km from Rajahmundry Railway station.

Accomodation: Forest Rest Houses at Rajahmundry, Maredumilli and Kannapuram. Inspection Bungalow at Rampachodavaram. Forest Guest House at V.R. Puram in Khammam district is also close to the sanctuary.

Contact: Divisional Forest Officer (WLM), Rajahmundry (Ph: 0883-2478643, 9440810044) or Forest Range Officer, Rampachodavaram (Ph: 08864-243705, 9440810238, 9440810235).

Pocharam Wildlife Sanctuary
(129.84 sqkm), Medak and Nizamabad Districts

Pocharam Wildlife Sanctuary is located in the bordering parts of Medak and Nizamabad Districts of Andhra Pradesh. Pocharam Lake in the sanctuary, which has a surface area of 9.12 sq km, is a home to many migratory birds like Bar-headed Geese, Brahminy Ducks, Painted and Open-billed Storks. Pocharam Forest was the favourite hunting ground of the Nizam until he declared it as a wildlife sanctuary in the early 20th century.

Forest type: Dry deciduous forest with patches of scrub and fairly large grassy plains, low hills and water pools.

Flora: Deciduous trees and thorny scrub with *Acacia,* poles of Axle Wood, Teak and *Terminalia* spp.

Fauna: The main faunal species are Leopard, Jungle Cat, Sloth Bear, Sambar, Chital, Four Horned Antelope, Nilgai, Chinkara, and birds like Pelicans, Flamingoes, Black Ibis, Brahminy Duck etc.

Best Season to Visit: October to May.

Accessibility: 120 km by road from Hyderabad. 40 km from Medak. Medak is well connected by road and there are frequent buses from Hyderabad. Private transport is also available.

Accomodation: Inspection Bungalow at Pocharam and Forest Rest House at Medak.

Contact: Divisional Forest Officer (WLM), Medak (Ph: 08452-222591, 9440810477).

Pranahita Wildlife Sanctuary
(136.02 sq km), Adilabad District

The Pranahita Wildlife Sanctuary is situated to the East of Kawal Sanctuary and North of the Godavari River in Adilabad district. Pranahita River, a tributary to Godavari, that forms the boundary between our state and Maharashtra flows along the eastern border of this sanctuary. It is home to the endangered Black Buck, Chinkara and Wolf. Pre-historic rock formations of the Deccan Plateau are a special tourist attraction here.

Forest type: The forest type is of Southern Tropical Dry Deciduous type, with patches of riverine forests along the river course.

Flora: Teak, *Lannea coromandelica*, Bamboo, Flame of the forest, *Terminalia spp* and *Anogeisus spp* are the commonly found tree species in Pranahita Sanctuary.

Fauna: Mammals like Tiger, Leopard, Jungle Cat, Jackal, Wild Dog, Sloth Bear, Common Langur, Rhesus Macaque, Four Horned Antelope, Palm Civet and Smooth Coated Indian Otter are found here. The avifauna includes aquatic birds like teals, storks, herons, kingfishers etc. The reptilian fauna includes Star Tortoise, Marsh Crocodile, Monitor Lizard, Common Krait, etc.

Best season to visit: November to April.

Accessibility: 70 km from Mancherial Railway station. 300 km. from Hyderabad by road.

Accomodation: Forest Rest House at Mancherial and Chennur.

Contact: Divisional Forest Officer, Jannaram (Ph: 08739-236224) or Divisional Forest Officer Mancherial, Adilabad (Ph.08736-252093) or FRO, Mancherial, Adilabad District (Ph. 08736-254752).

Pulicat Bird Sanctuary (500 sq km), Nellore District

Pulicat sanctuary is the second largest *brackish water lagoon* in India spread over two states of Andhra Pradesh and Tamil Nadu. It is formed out of backwaters of Bay of Bengal. The lake is rich in deposits of silica, lime deposits, gypsum and other minerals, supporting the largest flamingo nesting ground in the state.

Forest type: The forests surrounding Pulicat are primarily mangroves and littoral forests. The sanctuary area has some very significant remnant patches of Southern tropical dry evergreen forests.

Flora: Mangrove forests have plants like *Excoecaria agallocha*, *Aviciennia officinalis* and *Rhizophora apiculata*. The littoral forests have plants like *Spinifix littoralis*, *Ipomoea biloba* and *Solanum xanthocarpum*. Southern tropical dry evergreen forests have species like *Albizzia amara, Ficus tielea*, etc.

Fauna: The principal bird species that visit the Pulicat lake are the greater and lesser flamingoes and other birds including Spotbilled Pelicans, Painted Stork, Spoonbills, Grey Herons, teals, terns, gulls, Spotbilled Ducks, Painted Storks, a number of waders like Greenshanks, Spotted Redshanks, Golden Plover, Little Ringed Plover, Kentish Plover, Sandpipers, etc. The mammalian fauna includes Jungle Cat, Jackal, Wild Boar, etc. It also supports a rich diversity of aquatic fauna like silver pomfrets, white pomfrets, sable fish, prawns and other crustaceans, molluscs, coelenterates and plankton.

Best Season to Visit: October to March.

Accessibility: It is 10 km by road from Sullurpet Railway station, 50 km by road from Chennai on the Chennai-Kolkata road (N.H 5).

Contact: Divisional Forest Officer, Nellore (Ph: 9440810071, 08623242158).

Rajiv Gandhi Wildlife Sanctuary (Nagarjunasagar Srisailam Tiger Reserve) (3568 sq km), Guntur, Prakasam, Kurnool, Mahaboobnagar and Nalgonda Districts.

This is the largest tiger reserve in the country. The forest consists mainly of deep gorges and valleys, with River Krishna flowing through the land.

Forest type: Dry mixed deciduous forest, Dry deciduous scrub.

Flora: The plants like East Indian Satinwood (Bael), bamboo, teak, arjun and numerous medicinal plants like *Rauwolfia serpentina*, *Abrus precatorius*,etc. are present here.

Fauna: The forest is rich in bird species. Birds like Grey Hornbill, Red Spurfowl, Crested Hawk Eagle can be seen here. The mammals include Tiger, Leopard, Jackal, Wolf, Fox, Wild Dog, Sloth Bear, Ratel, Sambhar, Chital, Black Buck, Mouse Deer, Chowsingha, Nilgai, Giant Indian Squirrel and Tree Shrew. The reptilian fauna too is amazing with Marsh Crocodile, turtles, Russell's Viper and Saw-scaled Viper present.

Accessibility: 130 km by road from Hyderabad.

Best Season to Visit: October to May.

Accomodation: Forest Rest Houses and cottages at Srisailam, Mannanur, Atmakur,

Bairluty, Nagarjunasagar, Mancherial and Markapur. APTDC's Punnami and Ganga Sadan at Srisailam are also good resting places.

Contact: Field Director, Project Tiger, Sunnipenta, Srisailam, Kurnool District (Ph:08524-286089), D.F.O. Achampet (Ph: 08541-272136), D.F.O., Atmakur (Ph. 08517-283337), D.F.O., Nagarjunasagar (Ph. 08680-276877) , D.F.O. Markapur, Prakasam District (Ph. 08596-222082).

Rollapadu Wildlife Sanctuary (6.14 sqkm), Kurnool District

Rollapadu Wildlife Sanctuary is a very important sanctuary declared for the protection of one of the most beautiful and endangered birds in the world- Great Indian Bustard, endemic to the Indian sub-continent.

Forest type: The forest consists of open grassland interspersed with dry thorny bushes

Flora: *Gymnosporia montana*, *Ixora parviflora*, *Ziziphus* species, *Acacia* species. Various species of grasses with short, thorny bushes.

Fauna: Wolf, Fox, Jackal, Bonnet Macaque, Black Buck and Black-naped hare are the mammals present here. The reptiles are represented by the Indian cobra, Russell's viper etc. Besides the Great Indian Bustard, this sanctuary is home to the equally endangered, associate bird - the Lesser florican. The other bird life includes Pied Bushchat, Black-bellied Finch Lark, Syke's Crested Skylark, Red-winged Bushlark, Indian chestnut bellied sand grouse, Indian Courser, Richard's Pipit, White throated Silverbill, Spotted Owlet, Grey francolin, Yellow-throated sparrow, Pale Harrier, Short-toed Eagle, Lagger Falcon, White-eyed Buzzard, etc.

Best season to visit: October to April.

Accessibility: The Sanctuary is a 45 km drive away from Kurnool city.

Accomodation: Forest Rest House at Kurnool, Rollapadu and Inspection Bungalow at Nandikotkur.

Contact: Field Director, Project Tiger, Srisailam, Kurnool District (Ph. 08524-286089, 08596-222082, 9440810057) or Divisional Forest Officer , Atmakur (Ph: 08517-283337).

Sivaram Wildlife Sanctuary (29.81 sq km) , Adilabad and Karimnagar Districts

Located in the Adilabad and Karimnagar districts along river Godavari in Andhra Pradesh, this sanctuary falls in the perennial basin of River Godavari and is home to the marsh crocodile also known as mugger.

Forest type: Deciduous and mixed riverine forest in the Godavari river basin.

Flora: Riverine Forest Type mixed with Teak, Bamboo, Axle wood, Terminalias and Cassias.

Fauna: Leopard, Jungle Cat, Jackal, Fox, Sloth Bear, Wild Boar, Hanuman Langur, Rhesus Monkey, Sambar and Chital are the mammals present in the sanctuary. This sanctuary is known for its high population of Marsh Crocodiles. The Indian Rock Python is also present.

Best Season to Visit: November to May.

Accessibility: 10 km from Manthani , Karimnagar District and 50 km from Mancherial Railway station.
Accomodation: Forest Rest House at Mancherial and Eklaspur (Manthani).
Contact: Divisional Forest Officer (WLM), Jannaram, Adilabad district (Ph: 08739-236688) or Divisional Forest Officer, Karimnagar East Division (Ph: 0878-2243610)

Sri Lankamalleshwara Wildlife Sanctuary (464.42 sq km), Cuddapah District

The sanctuary, extending over Cuddapah and Poduttur forests, is the only place where the Jerdon's Courser is seen. This is an extremely endangered bird which was rediscovered after about 110 years. The sanctuary is cradled in the isolated Lankamalla hills replete with deep gorges and steep slopes.
Forest type: *Dry deciduous red sanders forests* on the hills and *scrub forests* in the plains.
Flora: Red sanders and Sandalwood are important species of this area. The *riparian (riverine) vegetation* is represented by Teak, Butter Tree, Taloora Lac Tree, Mangoes and *Carissa* bushes. Bamboo is intermixed with other vegetation.
Fauna: Leopard, Fox, Sloth Bear, Wild Boar, Sambar, Chital, Chowsinga, Nilgai, Grey Hornbill can be seen in the forests, while nightjars are common in the scrub.
Best season to visit: October to March.
Accessibility: The sanctuary is 60 km by road from Cuddapah town.
Accomodation: Forest Rest House at Siddavotam and Cuddapah.
Contact: Conservator of Forests, Kurnool (Ph: 08518-220241), Divisional Forest Officer, Prodattur (Ph: 08564-248018, 9440810073) or Forest Range Officer, Cuddapah (Ph: 08562-244583).

Sri Penusila Narasimha (Vligonda) Wildlife Sanctuary (1030.85 sq km), Nellore District.

Located in the Nellore and Cuddapah districts, this sanctuary protects two big reservoirs, Somasila and Kandaleru, and has rich, evergreen forests.
Forest type: Dry evergreen forest of Eastern Ghats with hilly slopes, low valleys.
Flora: Red Sanders, *Zizyphus xylopyrus*, *Terminaiia arjuna*, *Acacia spp, Cassia spp,* and *Carissa* bushes.
Fauna: Leopard, Jackal, Sloth Bear, Wild Boar, Sambar, Chital, Nilgai, Chowsingha are found here. A large number of reptiles and birds are also present here.
Best season to visit: July to March
Accessibility: This sanctuary is 50 km from Nellore by road.
Accomodation: Forest Guest House and Inspection Bungalow at Nellore.
Contact: Divisional Forest Officer, Nellore (Ph. 0861-2326393, 9440810052), Forest Range Officer, Nellore (Ph. 0861-232383).

BIRDS

Birds are beautiful to watch and fascinating to listen to. Many people enjoy trying to mimic their songs. Birds are useful neighbours. For example, swallows, drongos and many other birds are insectivores, helping us get rid of insect pests.There are many bird behaviours that you are familiar with such as bird calls, nesting and migration. Birds have a 'call' and a 'song'. Birds call to stay in touch while flying or they are used as alarms. Bird songs are special notes (usually in the breeding season) used by males in the breeding season to mark territories and attract females. Besides songs, birds use other courtship displays such as showing off their breeding plumage (in peacocks), mutual preening (in parakeets and barbets) or nuptial displays (acrobatic flights in Indian rollers and high jumps in Bengal florican).

Nesting is an important social activity in the life of birds. Many people make studying nests their hobby. This is called 'Caliology ' or 'Nidology'. Nests are built in strategic locations and have ingenious designs to defend against predators. The eggs too are interestingly coloured and marked for camouflage.

Once the breeding season ends and the nestlings have grown, the parent birds shed their feathers in a set pattern. Usually flight feathers are shed once a year while body feathers moult twice a year.

Bird migration has fascinated humans since time immemorial. Certain birds migrate halfway across the world every year with clockwork precision in search of suitable habitats - for feeding and for breeding. The urge to migrate is stimulated partly by season and partly due to an internal hormonal change.The regularity and accuracy of bird migrations has intrigued ornithologists. Not only do birds visit the same spots each year, they do so on nearly the same date! There is also a phenomenon of local migration which is governed by food supply.

Though we have generalised bird behaviour here, each species displays its own characteristic behaviour. For this reason, the study of bird diversity can be very rewarding. To understand the diversity among birds, it is important to classify them. In the 1750's, Carlos Linnaeus, a Swedish scientist, established a system or hierarchy of living organisms so that scientists all over the world could understand each other. Since then, the Linnaeus System has been, and is still being used and improvised upon today as new discoveries are made among groups of birds. The science of naming living organisms such as birds, is called "Taxonomy" and it can become quite complicated, but the basics are easy to understand.

All living organisms are divided into 5 Kingdoms: Plants, Fungi, Animals, Protista and Bacteria (the last two have to be seen through a microscope). The living members of the Animal (Animalia) Kingdom is divided into smaller groups called Phylum (singular) or Phyla (plural) which means a direct line of descent within a group and then its further divided into smaller groups called Classes. Classes are divided into even smaller (though still fairly large) groups called Orders. After categorizing the Orders, we have Families and sometimes Subfamilies. Within each Family/Subfamily, there are a number of Genera (plural for Genus) and within each Genus are a number of Species.

All birds fall in the class Aves of the Phylum Vertebrata of the Kingdom Animalia. The following table describes the bird orders and families that are represented in Andhra Pradesh.

The figures that follow the table will give you an idea of the parts of a bird, making it easier for you to understand bird descriptions and also to make notes of your own observations. There are also illustrations of the diferent kinds of beaks and feet in the bird world, that indicate not only bird diversity, but also give a clue of the bird's habits and habitats. These illustrations have been adapted from Salim Ali's 'Book of Indian Birds'.

There are over 500 species of birds in Andhra Pradesh. Many are very rare, such as the Jerdon's Courser. Population of a few others is declining alarmingly, such as that of vultures. Many agencies and organisations are making noteworthy efforts to study and conserve these endangered birds. In Andhra Pradesh, we have seventeen threatened birds. White Backed Vulture, Long Billed Vulture and Jerdon's Courser are critically endangered. The Great Indian Bustard and the Lesser Florican are endangered. Spotbilled Pelican, Lesser Adjutant, Great Spotted Eagle , Indian Skimmer and Yellow Throated Bulbul are vulnerable. Darter, Painted Stork, Oriental White Ibis, Ferruginous Pochard, Greater Grey-headed Fish Eagle, Pallid Harrier and the Black -bellied Tern are near-threatened. All these birds are mentioned in the IUCN Redlist.

This book does not describe all these threatened species, though a few do find mention within the pages. The reason is simple- our aim is to initiate bird watching with introduction to bird species that are more commonly seen in the wild. Each bird description has information on size, common English, Telugu and Hindi names. Most of the time, the Telugu names given are true vernacular names. But, as it often happens with vernacular names, many birds have got ignored in vernacular, or more than one species have the same name, or else, people have forgotten the original Telugu names and therefore nobody can relate to them anymore. In these cases, we have used direct translation of the English names, as used in "Birds of Southern India", by Grimmett, Inskipp and Inskipp.

Certain descriptions exclude information on breeding and nesting behaviour, for, these species do not breed in Andhra Pradesh and the reader might not come across nests or breeding behaviour of these species in this state.

We have illustrated different types of beaks and feet in birds. These charts have been reproduced with permission from Dr. Salim Ali's 'The Book of Indian Birds', 11th edition.

Useful Tips for Birdwatchers

Early morning is the best time for bird watching. Birds sing in the morning when you may identify them by their sound also. Evenings are also a good time.

Do not strain to look for birds in a forest. Let your eyes wander to detect movement.

Edges or eco-tones, where one type of landscape merges into another, are usually sites of higher activity, especially at dawn and dusk.

Birds need water. Streams, ponds, fountains, especially with protective cover at hand are all excellent spots for bird watching.

Forest birds tend to move in mixed flocks. When you spot such a flock, determine the flocks' direction, get ahead of them and wait for them to follow you. This way, you don't disturb them and you get more time to observe them.

Woodland birds hide when they sense movement. Sit quietly with your back to a tree, in a clearing and wait for birds to come to you.

If you are in an area that has ground-nesting birds, be careful not to step on their nests. You may crush their eggs!

Open waters, mud flats and salt marshes are very good places to watch waders (water birds).

Don't be prejudiced against the common birds. Enjoy all your birds. There aren't any 'better' or 'more exotic' species. If the birds are where you are, stay and watch them for you may not see any more that day!

Carry a good field guide, a notebook and a pair of binoculars (7 to 10 times magnification) with you, which would help you identify the birds you see. A micro-cassette recorder, camera or video recorder are other ways of capturing the joy of the sights and smells in your memory.

Try to record the most important aspects of behaviour of the birds you have spotted.

Format of field notebook:

Date	Start Time	End Time
Location	Habitat Type	Weather conditions

After noting these details, you may note the name of bird, body characteristics, colour description, number of birds, call or sound, flying habit, food preferences, and any other peculiarity.

Compare your findings with standard books or guides. Take the help of an expert to learn more. Write your report in a fair note book or on an excel worksheet in your computer for future use.

Do's and Don'ts for successful bird watching

Do's	Don't's
Always wear dull colored,cotton clothes-greens and browns.	Bright blue, red or orange clothes and noisy fabric are a strict no!
Always follow used roads and trails.	Never explore or destroy the natural habitat.
Go in small groups.	Avoid large groups, they are noisy.
Carry a good field guide on Indian birds with you.	Do not carry a book on foreign birds. It will confuse you.
Carry a note pad.	Avoid writing on loose pieces of paper.
Use light weight binoculars.	Do not go too close to the nests. Once frightened, birds may abandon their nests and this could set their breeding back a whole year.
Keep a safe distance from the birds.	
Take prior permission before you visit any private land.	

Orders of Class Aves	Families	Description
Falconiformes	Accipitridae Falconidae Pandionidae Acquilidae Gypidae	Eagles, vultures, kites, hawks, falcons and osprey
Anseriformes	Anatidae Dendrocygnidae	Waterfowl like ducks, geese etc
Apodiformes	Apodidae Hemiprocnidae	Swifts
Bucerotiformes	Bucerotidae	Hornbills
Caprimulgiformes	Caprimulgidae	Nightjars
Charadriiformes	Charadridae	Plovers and allies
Ciconiiformes	Anhingidae Ardeidae	Storks and allies
Columbiformes	Columbidae	Doves and pigeons
Coraciiformes	Alcedinidae Cerylidae Dacelonidae Halcyonidae Coraciidae Meropidae	Kingfishers, rollers and bee-eaters
Cuculiformes	Centropodidae Cuculidae	Cuckoos
Galliformes	Phasianidae	Fowls and pheasants
Gruiformes	Gruidae Otididae Rallidae	Cranes, bustards and rails
Passeriformes	Aegithalidae Alaudidae	Passerines and larks
Pelecaniformes		Pelicans and allies
Phoenicopteriformes		Flamingos
Piciformes	Megalaimidae Picidae	Woodpeckers and barbets
Podicipediformes		Grebes
Psittaciformes	Psittacidae	Parrots and allies
Pteroclidiformes		Sandgrouse
Strigiformes	Strigidae Batrachostomidae Caprimulgidae Eurostopodidae	Owls, frogmouths and nightjars
Upupiformes	Upopidae	Hoopoe

PARTS OF A BIRD

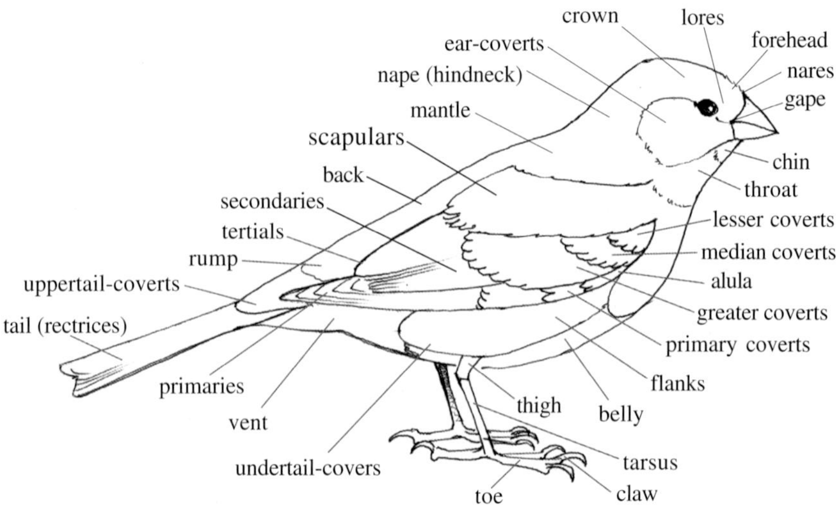

TYPES OF BILLS

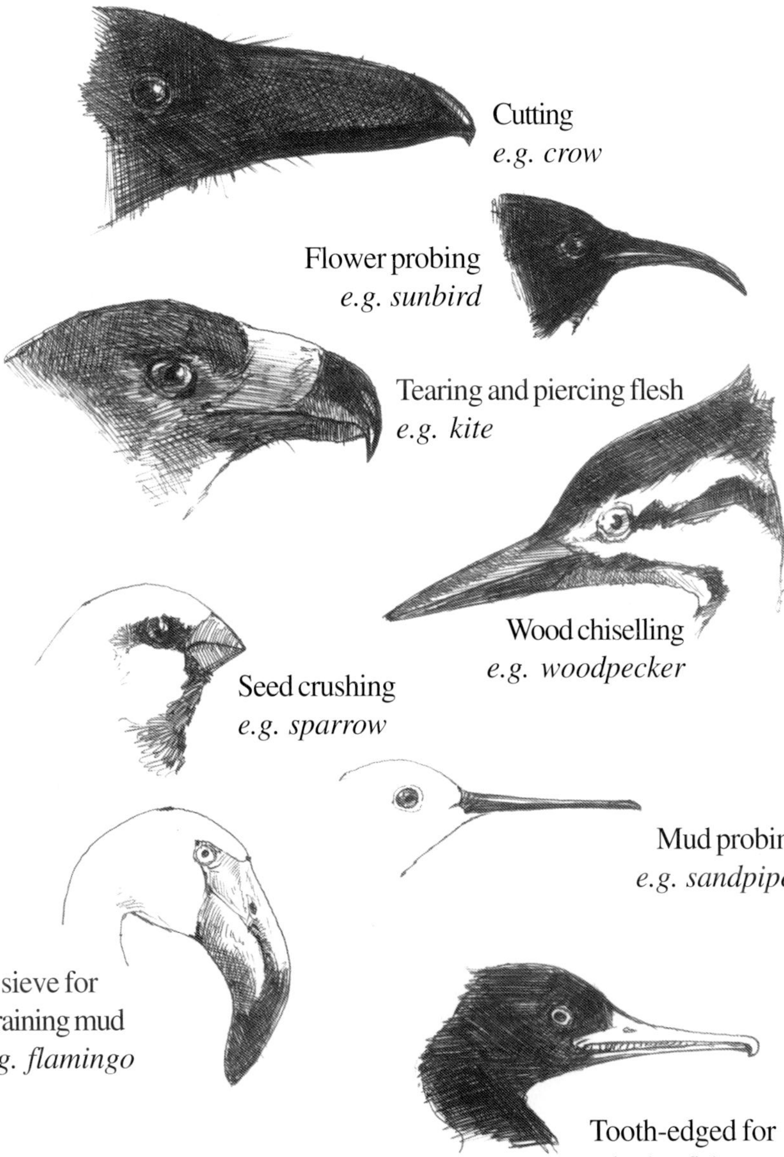

Cutting
e.g. crow

Flower probing
e.g. sunbird

Tearing and piercing flesh
e.g. kite

Wood chiselling
e.g. woodpecker

Seed crushing
e.g. sparrow

Mud probing
e.g. sandpiper

A sieve for straining mud
e.g. flamingo

Tooth-edged for gripping fish
e.g. cormorant

Source: Ali, Salim, The Book of Indian Birds, 11th ed, BNHS.

TYPES OF CLAWS

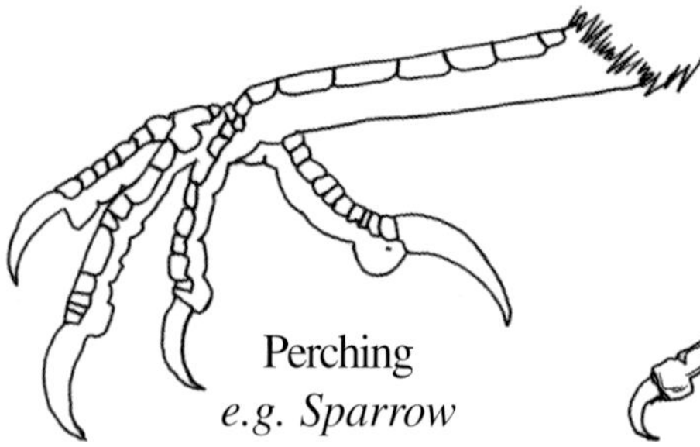

Perching
e.g. Sparrow

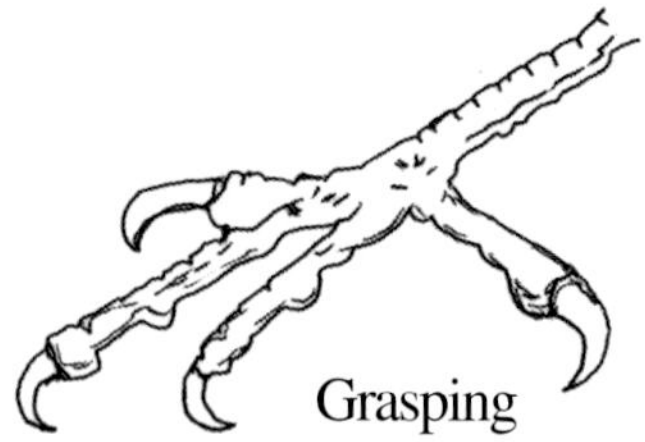

Grasping
and striking prey
e.g. Hawk

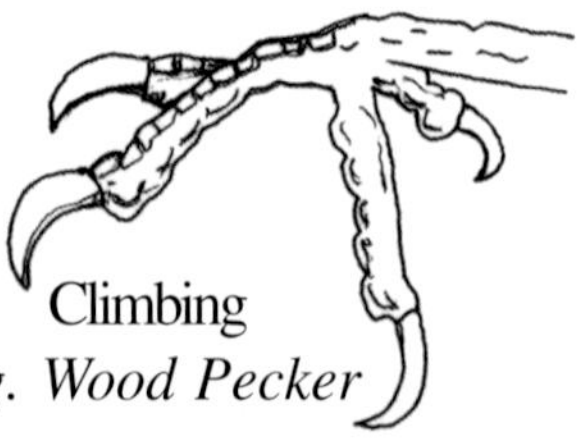

Climbing
e.g. Wood Pecker

Clinging
e.g. Swift

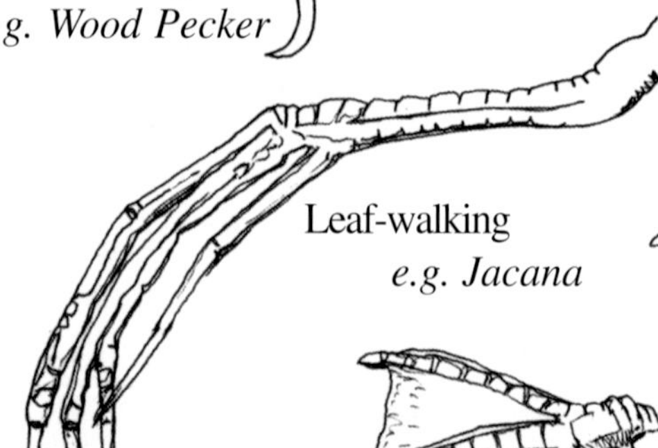

Leaf-walking
e.g. Jacana

Running
e.g. Courser

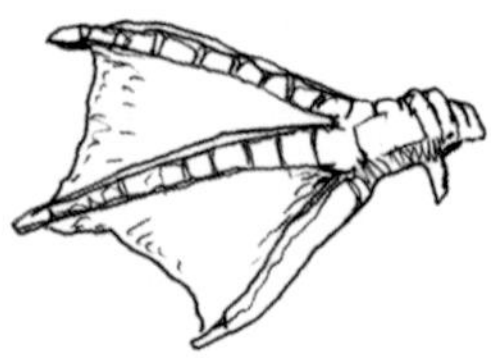

Swimming
e.g. Duck

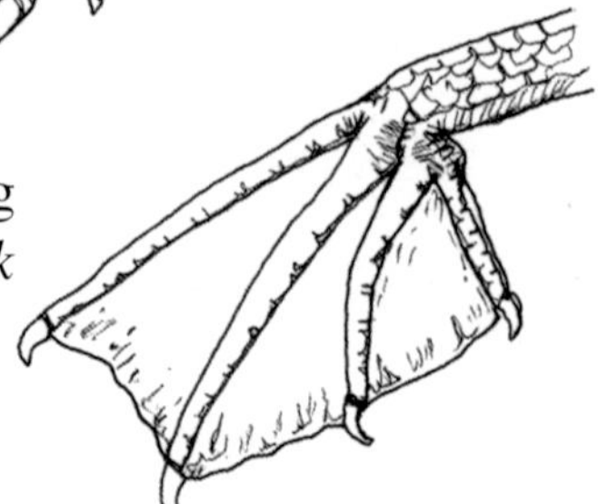

Swimming
e.g. Coot

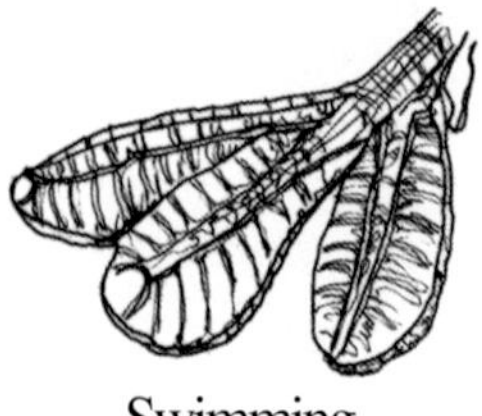

Swimming
e.g. Grebe

Source: Ali, Salim, The Book of Indian Birds, 11th ed, BNHS.

Little Cormorant *Phalacrocorax niger*
Local name: Chinna Neeti Kaki (Telugu), Pan-kowwa (Hindi) Size : 51 cm

This bird is frequently found in the vicinity of water bodies, perched on a rock or a low-lying branch, spreading out its wings. It swims low in the water with only the head, neck and upper part of its back exposed. This cormorant is almost completely black, except for a small white patch on the throat. The sharply hooked beak is ideal for holding fish and the bird hunts for these by diving into the water. The nesting season is between November and February. The Little Cormorant nests in a mixed colony with other water birds such as egrets and storks.

The nest is a shallow platform of twigs.

Oriental Darter *Anhinga melanogaster*
Local name:Paamu Baathu (Telugu), Panwa (Hindi) Size : 85 - 90 cm

This dark, long-necked bird is often spotted in water bodies, swimming with most of its body submerged or sitting on a nearby rock or tree stump holding out its wings. The neck and the head stick out above the water, giving it the appearance of a snake and thus the name, snake-bird. The darter is an expert underwater swimmer and catches fish by spearing them with its sharp beak. The nesting season is between June and March and the nest is part of a mixed colony of cormorants, egrets, herons and ibises.

Little Grebe *Tachybaptus ruficollis*
Local name: Chinna Munugudi Kodi (Telugu), Pandubi (Hindi) Size : 25 - 29 cm

This miniature grebe is easy to spot in any pond or lake despite its drab colours. It has silky underparts and the breeding male sports a chestnut neck. It is an excellent diver, hunting underwater for small fish, tadpoles, frogs and insects. The nesting season is between April and October. The nest is a pad of weeds and rushes made on floating vegetation. The bird covers its eggs with weeds before leaving the nest.

Purple Heron *Ardea purpurea*
Local name: Yerranarayana Konga (Telugu), Lal Anjan (Hindi) Size : 78 - 90 cm

This is a sleek heron – bluish grey above, with a thin neck.Crown, crest and cheek stripes are black.Sides of the head are chestnut. Usually seen singly at ponds and lakes, with good vegetation cover. It is active in the early mornings and evenings, keeps to tall vegetation in the water, feeding on fish, frogs, snakes, etc. The nesting season is practically through out the year. The nest is a platform of twigs built in trees, usually in those standing in water.

Grey Heron *Ardea cinerea*
Local Name: Narayana Konga (Telugu), Anjan (Hindi) Size : 90 - 98 cm

A slim, tall, ashy grey bird, with a white head and neck. Black plumes on the head make a fine recumbent crest. Usually found singly, wading or standing attentively in ponds and lakes, looking for frogs and fish, which are struck at lighting speed with its dagger sharp bill. When disturbed, it utters a hoarse croak – but otherwise has no distinct call. The nesting season is between November and March. The nest is a platform made of twigs lined with grass, usually built in a mixed heronry.

Indian Pond Heron *Ardeola grayii*
Local Name: Guddi Konga (Telugu), Andha Bagla (Hindi) Size : 40 - 45 cm

A small, stocky, dull coloured heron usually spotted sitting hunched up in water-filled ditches, marshy patches, ponds and lakes. Reveals white wings in flight. In the breeding season, this usually drab-coloured bird sports maroon filamentous plumes on the back and a white crest. It stands motionless at the water's edge waiting patiently for frogs, fish or water insects to swim by. The unsuspecting prey is jabbed with the beak and eaten in a flash. This deceptive feeding style gave rise to the Telugu phrase "*Konga Japam*" (stork's penance) used in reference to acts of deception performed under the guise of a saintly public face. The nesting season is between November and January. The nest is an untidy twig platform built in a large tree in the company of nests of other water birds such as egrets.

Little Egret *Egretta garzetta*
Local name: Chinna Tella Konga (Telugu), Karchia Bagla (Hindi) Size : 55 - 65 cm

This slender, snow-white egret has a black beak, black legs and yellow feet, and sports a crest of filament like plumes in the breeding season. Unlike the cattle egret, this egret is usually found close to wetlands and water bodies. This bird is normally silent except for the throaty squawk it gives when disturbed and various noises it makes in nesting colonies. It roosts communally. The nesting season is between November and February. The nest is a twig platform built usually in a mixed colony where other water birds such as cattle egrets, pond herons, etc., also nest.

Black-crowned Night-Heron
Nycticorax nycticorax
Local name: Chinta Vakhi (Telugu), Waak (Hindi)
Size : 58 - 65 cm

A stocky, small heron – ashy grey above, white below, with a black bill and bright red eyes. Mostly active at night – but can be spotted during the day roosting in trees. The young are brownish with white spots, quite unlike the adults. Towards the evening it leaves the roost to find food (fish, water insects, crabs, etc.) in ponds and lakes. The nesting season is between December and February. The nest is a twig platform built in a large tree in the company of several other nests.

Cattle Egret *Bubulcus ibis*
Local name: Santi Konga (Telugu), Gai-bagla (Hindi) Size : 48 - 53 cm

This is our most common egret. The yellow bill and loose jowls distinguish it from the black-beaked little egret, when in its non-breeding pure white plumage. In the breeding season the bird dons an orange-buff plumage on the head, neck and back. Mostly seen following grazing cattle, seeking insects disturbed from the grass. Several dozens gather at dusk to roost in tall trees. The nesting season is between November and March. The untidy twig platform nest is built usually in a mixed colony where several other water birds such as cormorants, pond herons, etc., also nest.

Painted Stork

Mycteria leucocephala

Local name: Yerrakala Konga (Telugu), Dokh (Hindi)

Size : 93 - 100 cm

Large stork with a heavy yellow bill, unfeathered waxy yellow face and white plumage with delicate rose-pink on shoulders and wings. Wings have greenish-black markings.Seen in inland water bodies sitting hunched up or moving in shallow water seeking fish, frogs and snakes with its partly submerged beak. Indulges in cooperative feeding where birds form a loose arc and wade through shallow water, driving fish towards the shore, feeding as they go. Breeding season is at the end of the monsoon. Nest is a platform of twigs lined with leaves and straw, placed in a tree in a large mixed colony.

Asian Openbill-Stork

Anastomus oscitans

Local name: Terapimukku Konga (Telugu), Gunghil (Hindi)

Size : 68 cm

A white stork with black wings and a distinct bill that has arching mandibles and a narrow open gap in the beak. Frequents lakes and marshes, singly or in small groups. Wades in shallow water probing the muddy bottom for food with its open beak. Also searches for food on bare surroundings of lakes. Feeds on molluscs, crustaceans, frogs and fish. The breeding season begins in the monsoon. Nests in a mixed colony with other birds.Nest is a platform of twigs, lined with leaves placed in a tree.

White-necked Stork *Ciconia episcopus*

Local name: Wadumi konga (Telugu), Laglag (Hindi) Size : 75 - 92 cm.

A glistening black stork with a white neck , abdomen and vent, reddish legs, black beak and cap.Found singly or in small flocks on marshy ground, paddies or wet grasslands. It feeds on frogs, fish, reptiles, crabs, mollusks, insects, etc. Nesting season is throughout the year. The nest is a platform of twigs lined with grass, etc., placed singly on the top of a tall tree.

Oriental White Ibis *Threskiornis melancephalus*
Local name: Nalla kankanami (Telugu), Safed baza (Hindi) Size : 75 cm

A large white marsh bird, with the characteristic curved beak of the ibises, and a black head. Found usually in small parties in marshes and near water bodies. They hunt for insects, fish and frogs by probing in the muddy water with the beak held partly open. The nesting season is between November and February. The nest is a platform of twigs, and is built in a mixed heronry shared with egrets, spoonbills, cormorants, etc.

Black Ibis *Pseudibis papillosa*
Local name: Nallatala Kanakam (Telugu), Baza (Hindi) Size : 68 cm

A large black marsh bird, with a prominent, curved beak, red legs, red patch on the naked head and white patches on the shoulders. Usually found in small groups near dried up marshes, fallow fields and other such drier habitats. The nesting season is between November and December. The nest is a large cup made of twigs, straw, feathers, etc., built singly high up in a tree.

Eurasian Spoonbill *Platelea leucorodia*
Local name: Teddumoothi Konga (Telugu), Chamack baza (Hindi) Size : 80-90 cm

A snow white bird with black legs and prominent spatulate bill. Found in marshes, jheels,estuarine mudflats and mudbanks in rivers. They hunt for tadpoles, frogs,snails,insects and vegetable matter by raking up the bottom mud with partly open bills sweeping in semi-circles. The nesting season is from July to November. The nest is a massive stick platform in a mixed heronry.

Greater Flamingo *Phoenicopterus ruber*
Local name: Samudrapu chiluka (Telugu), Rajhans (Hindi) Size : 125 - 145 cm

Found in small flocks in shallow waters and estuaries. Long legs, long neck, rosy-white body, heavy pink bent bill, characteristic of flamingoes. Black tipped scarlet wings visible in flight.Feeds in shallow water, with head completely immersed, sieving out food (small molluscs, larvae, crustaceans, seeds of water plants, etc.) Flocks fly in a V formation. Breeds in Gujarat (Great Rann of Kutch) in September-October and February-April. Migrates in large numbers to Pulicat Lake where a Flamingo Festival is held in February.

Lesser Flamingo *Phoenicopterus minor*
Local name: Vankaramoothi konga (Telugu), Chhota rajhans (Hindi)
Size : 80 - 90 cm

Pink bird with a blackish beak where the upper mandible does not cover the lower mandible completely. It has crimson and black underwings. Found in large groups especially in very salty, shallow waters. Walks or swims in shallow water moving its head from side to side sieving algae. Breeds in Gujarat (in the Great Rann of Kutch) in June-July extending into January-February. Migrates locally and is found in small numbers at Pulicat Lake in winter.

Spotbilled Pelican *Pelecanus philippensis*
Local name: Chukkalamukku chinakabaathu (Telugu), Hawasil (Hindi) Size: 140 cm

Usually found in groups in large lakes, coastal lagoons and estuaries. The grey pelican has a brown nuchal crest, short legs, webbed feet and a dull purplish bag attached to its enormous bill. Grey-brown tail , spotted bill and dull black wing quills are diagnostic. Fishes either singly or in groups. Birds swim in a semi-circle, driving fish before them into the shallow water by splashing their wings. Fish are scooped up in their pouched beaks. Nests between September and April in mixed colonies with other water birds. Nest is made of large twigs, lined in straw and reeds, etc. in large trees. Breeds in the colonies at Nelapattu and Telineelapuram in substantial numbers.

Brahminy Shelduck *Tadorna ferruginea*
Local name: Bapana baatu (Telugu), Chakwa (Hindi) Size : 61 - 67 cm

This attractive rusty-orange goose-like duck is a winter visitor to our state from the Himalayas and beyond. It usually feeds by grazing on banks of rivers and lakes; also by wading in shallows, dabbling and upending. It feeds on vegetable matter, molluscs, crustaceans, insects, fish and reptiles. It returns to its summer home for nesting in summer.

Spot-billed Duck *Anas poecilorhyncha*
Local name: Mukkuchukka baatu (Telugu), Garam-pai, Gugral (Hindi) Size : 58 - 63 cm

The yellow-tipped black bill gives this large resident dabbling duck its name. Usually found in pairs or in small flocks at freshwater marshes, tanks and pools with good emergent vegetation. Feeds by dabbling, head-dipping, upending, and walking about, in the marsh vegetation. The nesting season is between July and December. The nest is built with grass and weeds on the ground among dense bank side vegetation or in a marsh.

Red-crested Pochard *Rhodonessa rufina* Local name: Yerratala chiluvu (Telugu), Lal-sir (Hindi) Size : 53 - 57 cm

The male of this striking migrant duck has a rich chestnut-orange crested head and a bright red bill. This diving duck feeds on shoots and roots of water plants, molluscs, crustaceans, insects, etc., usually by diving and sometimes by upending and head-dipping. Usually found in large tanks with plenty of aquatic vegetation.

Comb Duck *Sarkidiornis melanotos*
Local name: Juttu chiluva (Telugu), Nakta (Hindi) Size : 56 - 76 cm

This large, stocky resident duck gets its name from the fleshy 'comb' the male sports at the base of the bill in the breeding season. It is a glossy, blue-black duck with white underparts and a white head and neck speckled with black. Water bodies with plenty of aquatic vegetation are its favourite haunts. Usually found in small flocks grazing in marshes and wet grasslands. Also wades and dabbles in shallow water. It perches easily on trees. The nesting season is between July and September. The nest is located in the hollow of a tree, usually located close to water.

Lesser Whistling-duck
Dendrocygna javanica
Local name: Eelavesi chinnachiluva (Telugu), Seelhi (Hindi) Size : 42 cm

This resident duck is commonly seen in flooded grasslands and paddy fields, freshwater marshes, shallow ponds and lakes with plenty of emergent vegetation. It is pale brown and maroon-chestnut in colour. It roosts in the daytime by perching on trees or rests on tanks. It feeds at night in flooded rice fields, etc., by grazing, dabbling in shallow water and by diving in deep water. The call is a *whi-whee* whistle, uttered when in flight. The nesting season is generally during the monsoon. The nest is generally made in a tree hollow or fork with twigs, grasses and leaves.

Cotton Teal
Nettapus coromandelianus
Local name: Parja (Telugu), Giria, Girja (Hindi) Size : 36 -37 cm

This is the smallest of our resident ducks usually found in all inland water bodies. Male glossy black above, white head, neck and underparts, prominent black collar and white wing bar. Female and non-breeding male paler, without collar or wing bar. It is a swift flier and a good diver. The call is a peculiar clucking, uttered in flight. It feeds mainly on floating vegetation and on insects by dabbling (surface feeding). It nests between July and September. The nest is made of grass and feathers in a natural hollow located in a tree trunk close to water.

Northern Pintail
Anas acuta
Local name: Sooditoka baatu (Telugu), Seenkh par (Hindi)
Size : 51 - 56 cm

The male of this dabbling duck sports long, pointed tail feathers in the breeding season. It also has a chocolate-coloured head with white stripes running down the sides of the neck. The female is dull coloured without the 'pin-tail'. This duck is a winter visitor to our country and flocks water bodies in large numbers. It feeds largely at night and in the early morning in marshes and flooded paddy fields. It can often be seen feeding by "up-ending", wherein it tilts its body into the water so that half the body is in and the tail points to the sky! It does not nest in our country.

Northern Shoveller
Anas clypeata
Local name: Chamchamooti baatu (Telugu), Tidari (Hindi) Size : 44 - 52 cm

This is a dabbling (surface feeding) duck with a long unmistakable shovel-like bill. It is a winter visitor and is found in pairs, and small and large flock in shallow fresh water bodies such as lakes, ponds, tanks, rivers, etc. The male's glistening green head and clean white chest help in identifying it from afar. It feeds by sweeping the bill from side to side while swimming, sifting the water for minute organisms and aquatic seeds. It also upends or fully immerses its head and neck while swimming, and sometimes feeds by wading and by diving.

Bar-headed Goose
Anser indicus

The two black bands on the white head are diagnostic. This is a winter visitor seen on large lakes and rivers. Spends the day on sandbanks in water bodies and feeds at night in fields and grasslands along the waterside. The honking is a musical, tantalising, *aang, aang*.

Changeable Hawk-Eagle *Spizaetus cirrhatus*
Local name: Juttu bhairi (Telugu), Shah baaz (Hindi)
Size : 61 - 72 cm

This is a large, broad-winged eagle found in various confusing colour phases. It has a prominent crest. It is brown above, white below with black or brown longitudinal streaks on the underparts.This bird is silent except in the breeding season (November-June) when it gives out an ascending series of high-pitched whistles "*ki-ki-ki-ki-ki-ki-ki-ki-ki-kee*". Spends most of the day perched upright on a tree, usually near a clearing, on the look out for its prey – ground birds and small mammals. The prey is swooped upon and taken away, held in its powerful talons. The nest is a large platform of sticks and twigs lined with leaves placed 12-30 metres up in a forest tree.

Crested Serpent Eagle *Spilornis cheela*
Local name: Nalla pamulu gadda (Telugu), Furj baaz (Hindi)
Size : 56 - 74 cm

This dark brown eagle with a prominent black and white crest is a bird of the forest and well-wooded country, especially partial to high rainfall areas. It has a habit of soaring over the forest, usually in pairs, the birds calling to each other in a high-pitched "*kek-kek-kek-kek-kee*". In flight, a white bar on the tail and two white bars on the wings are visible.It spends most of its time perched upright on a forest tree. The crest is raised when alarmed. Snakes, rodents, lizards and small birds form part of its prey. The nesting season is between December and June. The nest is made of sticks and twigs, and is built high up in a forest tree, usually near a stream.

Short-toed Snake-Eagle *Circaetus gallicus*
Local name: Pamulu gadda (Telugu), Saampmaar (Hindi)
Size : 62- 67 cm

This thick-set eagle has a large, owlish head. When perched the wing-tips reach the tail-end and the long unfeathered legs are prominent. This bird frequents dry plains, stony foothills and cultivated land. The call is mainly heard in the breeding season and has been described as "*pieeou, pieeou*" as well as "*quo-quo-quo*". It spends most of its time soaring, scanning the ground for snakes, lizards, frogs, small rodents and large insects from a height of about 15-30 metres, occasionally hovering against the wind. When the prey is spotted, it plunges onto it almost vertically. The nesting season is between December and March. The nest is a platform of twigs and sticks concealed in a medium sized tree.

Western Marsh Harrier
Circus aeruginosus
Local name: Tellatala pilligadda (Telugu), Safed Sira (Hindi) Size : 48 - 58 cm.

This winter visitor frequents marshes, lakes, flooded paddy fields, etc. Male is dark brown with a pale rufous head, neck, breast, silver-grey tail and wings, primaries black. It glides a few metres above the ground looking for prey, occasionally flapping its wings. When the prey is spotted, it drops down swiftly to make a catch, sometimes drowning its prey underwater. It feeds on frogs, fish, small mammals, snakes, lizards, small birds, etc. It often perches on the ground for long periods. It also roosts in groups on the ground in fallow fields.

Montagu's Harrier
Circus pygargus
Local name: Pilligadda (Telugu), Dastamal (Hindi) Size : 43 - 47 cm.

This winter visitor frequents scrub-covered plains, cultivation, foothills, grasslands and edges of marshes. It is a grey-brown hawk with a grey throat, breast, white abdomen with chestnut shaft stripes and narrow black transverse wing bars diagnostic. The female is brown, with a buff-coloured owl-like ruff. Habits are similar to those of the Marsh Harrier, though it hunts over land. One of the largest roosts of this species is in Rollapadu Great Indian Bustard Sanctuary, Kurnool district.

Black-winged Kite *Elanus caeruleus*
Local name: Adavi Ramadasu (Telugu), Kapassi (Hindi) Size : 31 - 35 cm.

A smart, grey and white bird of prey, with bright red eyes and black "*kajal*" marks. Black patches in the shoulder visible in flight.Usually seen perched on telephone wires or poles on the look out for mice, lizards and large insects. It has the habit of frequently raising and lowering its tail when perched. Also frequently hovers in mid-air, scanning the ground for prey. The nesting season is throughout the year. The nest is an untidy twig structure lined with roots and grass built in a small tree.

Brahminy Kite *Haliastur indus*
Local name: Bapana gadda (Telugu), Brahmani Cheel (Hindi)
Size : 48 cm.

A bright, rusty-red kite with white head, neck and chest. Supposed to be the "*Garuda*" of Hindu mythology. Frequents the vicinity of water bodies and moves further away only in the monsoon. Food includes scavenged offal, fish, frogs, small snakes and termites caught in the air. The nesting season is between December and April. The nest is a loose platform of twigs lined with leaves built in a large tree near the water.

Black Kite *Milvus migrans*
Local name:Mala gadda (Telugu), Cheeel (Hindi)
Size : 55 - 68.5 cm.

Our most common kite. A large, dark brown bird with a deeply forked tail. At home in cities and towns. Easily recognised by its forked tail. Roosting in large numbers on large buildings and on trees in parks. Thrives as a scavenger in market places and at garbage dumps, hence also called pariah kite. Also eats earthworms, winged termites, lizards, mice, young birds, etc. The familiar call is described as musical "*ewe-wir-wir-wir*". Builds a large nest of twigs and rubbish in tall trees, buildings, etc.

Osprey *Pandion haliaetus*
Local name: Koramein gadda (Telugu), Machhlimaar (Hindi) Size : 55 - 58 cm.

This is a dark brown bird with a brown and white head, and white under parts having a brown band across the breast. This winter visitor is generally found in the vicinity of large inland water bodies and along the seacoast, perched on a dead tree or rock in or near the water. It scans the water surface, flying at a height of about 50 to 100 feet, occasionally hovering. On spotting a fish, it plunges down, strikes the water (often making a shallow dive), and catches the fish with its talons. It does not seem to breed in our country.

Indian White-backed Vulture *Gyps bengalensis*
Local name: Tella veepa borava (Telugu), Giddh (Hindi) Size : 75 - 85 cm.

Once our most common vulture, its declining numbers are now a cause of deep concern. Black-brown body, with a thin, naked face and neck. White back visible when seated or banking in flight. Feeds on carrion and scavenges on rubbish at garbage heaps and on the outskirts of villages and towns. Can also be seen effortlessly soaring high in the afternoon sky. Roosts communally. The nesting season is between October and March. The nest is a large untidy platform of sticks in a large tree.

Egyptian Vulture *Neophron percnopterus*
Local name: Tella Borava (Telugu), Giddh (Hindi) Size : 60 - 70 cm.

A dirty white vulture with black wing quills and a naked yellow face. Found in open country, often near human habitations. Soars about or perches near villages or at rubbish dumps, recognisable by its wedge-shaped tail. When on the ground, it walks with a waddling gait. Feeds on rubbish, human excrement, carcasses and also on frogs and insects. The nesting season is between February and May. The nest is a platform of twigs and rubbish placed on a ledge on rocks or in ruins or in a large tree.

Shikra *Accipiter badius*
Local name: Jaledegu (Telugu), Shikra (Hindi) Size : 30 - 36 cm.

This lightly built hawk is seen singly or in pairs in urban and suburban areas and lightly wooded country. Its call is a loud, harsh *titu-titu*, similar to that of a Black Drongo. It perches on the branch of a tree on the look out for prey that it catches by surprise. Rodents, birds, lizards, frogs, large insects, etc., are hunted and eaten. The breeding season is between January and June, at the beginning of which the birds indulge in circling display flights in the sky. The nest is a platform made of twigs in a tree.

Common Kestrel ***Falco tinnunculus***
Local name: Todala moochidega (Telugu), Karontiya (Hindi)
Size : 32 - 35 cm.

The male has a grey head, grey tail, brick red upper parts, light coloured under parts with brown markings. The female has rufous upper parts, head, neck and tail streaked with black. This slender falcon is a winter visitor and is usually found in open country perched upright on a post or branch. Its method of hunting involves scanning the ground for prey (mice, lizards, large insects) while hovering in mid-air with rapidly beating wings and fanned tail. Nesting season is from February to April. The nest is made on a ledge, cliff or crevice using twigs, roots, rags and other rubbish.

Painted Francolin *Francolinus pictus*
Local name: Kakera kanju/ kamsu (Telugu), Kak teetar (Hindi) Size : 31 cm.

This is a brownish-black partridge, profusely spotted and barred with white, wings and head chestnut coloured. White throat in females. It is commonly encountered in pairs or small parties in scrub country and in cultivation – usually in the vicinity of water. Roosts in trees and often perches on them even during the day. The call is a high-pitched "*chik-cheek-cheek-keray*". The nesting season coincides with the monsoon – and is between June and September. The nest is a shallow grass-lined scrape on the ground under a bush or on bunds in cultivation.

Grey Francolin *Francolinus pondicerianus*
Local name: Boodidarangu kanju/ kamsu (Telugu), Safed Teetar (Hindi) Size : 33 cm.

This is a plump, stub-tailed, greyish ground bird. It sports a rufous-buff and black necklace. The male has a pointed spur on each leg. It is commonly seen in pairs or in small parties in dry open country and in cultivation or waiting on the sides of highways, so it may scurry across when the road is empty (though it may be heard more often than seen). It feeds in a typical hen-like fashion scratching the ground for grains and insects. The call is a high-pitched musical "*kateetar-kateetar*" or "*pateela-pateela*". Nesting is between March and October but varies locally. The nest is a grass-lined scrape on the ground in scrub jungle, cultivation, etc.

Rain Quail *Coturnix coromandelica*
Local name: Nallabora elisey (Telugu), China buter (Hindi) Size : 18 cm.

This is a plump, squat almost tailless pale brown bird with black coloured upper breast and upper belly. It is usually found in pairs or in small parties in cultivation, grassland and scrub jungle. The call is a musical, metallic, high-pitched, quick-repeated "*whit-whit*" usually heard in the mornings and evenings. Between March and October (and particularly after the monsoon in June) – the breeding season, the call is also heard at night. The nest is a scrape in the open under a bush, in thin grass or standing crops.

Indian Peafowl *Pavo cristatus*
Local name: Nemali (Telugu), Mor (Hindi) Size : 180 - 230 cm.

This well-known bird is usually found in pairs or in small parties. Neck, crest feathers and breast are blue in male and metallic green in female. Wings are rufous brown, upperparts are brown and heavily marked. Male sports a magnificient glossy green train of elongated feathers with ocelli. It is usually found in light forest. The call is a loud "*kee-ow, kee-ow, kee-ow*", repeated 6-8 times. It roosts on large trees and descends to the ground to search for food (grains, vegetable shoots, insects, lizards, snakes, etc.) in the early mornings and late afternoons.In the breeding season a party may comprise of one male and 3-5 females. In the non-breeding season males remain in separate parties from the females and their young. The nesting season is between January and September, though it varies locally. The nest is a scrape made on the ground in dense undergrowth, lined with sticks and leaves.

Grey Junglefowl *Gallus sonneratii*
Local name: Tella adavikodi (Telugu), Jungli murga (Hindi) Size : 70 - 80 cm.

Male has a red comb and wattles, grey mottled gold and black neck plumes, black underparts, lustrous black-green sickle shaped tail. The female is brown, heavily streaked, with rufous underparts. Found singly, in pairs or in small parties in the undergrowth of forests and scrub jungle. Roosts in trees or bamboo clumps. Feeds on grain, shoots, tubers, berries, insects, etc. The male's crowing call is a loud *kuk-ka-kurruk-ka*, repeated at regular intervals, especially during early mornings and late evenings. The nesting season is between February and May. The nest is a shallow scrape on the ground in dense undergrowth or is made of twigs in a tree.

Great Indian Bustard *Ardeotis nigriceps*
Local name: Batta meka pakshi (Telugu), Sohan, Hoonkana (Hindi) Size : 92 - 122 cm.

The habitat of this endangered species is open grassland interspersed with cultivation. It is a heavy ground bird usually found in scattered groups of 3 or 4. This very large bustard has a grey or white neck, black crown and crest, brown upperparts and black wing coverets spotted with white. The male is one-third taller than the female and has a black breast band. It feeds on grains and shoots of crops, insects, lizards, etc. The nesting season is between March and September. The nest is a shallow depression at the base of a bush. A sanctuary for this magnificent bird has been established at Rollapadu in Kurnool district.

Lesser Florican *Sypheotides indica*
Local name: Nela nemmali (Telugu), Barsati charaz (Hindi). Size : 46 - 51 cm.

This is a slim bird with a long, black, slender neck, black underparts, white wing coverets, sandy, cinnamon-buff upperparts, heavily stippled. The breeding male sports attractive spatula-tipped head plumes. Females and juveniles are brown.This florican is mainly found in India but is a summer visitor to Pakistan. Found singly or in scattered pairs in dry grasslands with scattered bushes, cotton and millet crops. It feeds on green shoots, grains, seeds, beetles, etc. The breeding season is between July and October. The male is territorial.Mating display is unique, in that it jumps up and down at one place, so that it is visible above the grass. The nest is a bare patch in short grass or crops.

Common Coot *Fulica atra*
Local name: Nalabuli kodi (Telugu), Dasari (Hindi). Size : 36 - 38 cm.

This resident slaty-black rail is commonly encountered in our lakes. The white bill and frontal shield are what make coots so easy to identify. The toes are elongated and fringed on each side with a broad, scalloped membrane – an adaptation that helps in being a good swimmer. Winter brings in a number of migratory coots from central and western Asia – this explains the sudden spurt in their winter numbers. When disturbed, coots take off, half-running and half-flying on the water. They feed on grass, paddy shoots, waterweeds, insects, etc. The nesting season is between July and August. The nest is a large heap of rushes or other water plants generally anchored to a reed bed. Though placed slightly above water level, it is often destroyed by rising water levels due to monsoonal rains.

Common Moorhen *Gallinula chloropus*
Local name: Jambu kodi (Telugu), Jal murghi (Hindi). Size : 32 - 35 cm.

A dark-coloured water bird with a bright red shield at the forehead and base of the bill. Usually found in pairs near small well-vegetated water bodies. While swimming it bobs its head up and down and flicks up the tail to show white under tail coverts. Flies low over the water, head and neck stretched out and legs trailing behind. Calls include "*kurr-ik, kark, cuk – cuk – cuk, kook – kook*," etc. Feeds on insects, worms, molluscs, and parts of water plants. The nesting season is between June and September. The nest is a mass of water plants on the ground or in a low shrub close to water.

Purple Moorhen *Porphyrio (porphyrio) poliocephalus*
Local name: Udi chenchu kodi (Telugu), Kharim (Hindi) Size : 45 - 50 cm.
An attractive purple-coloured bird with a red-shielded forehead and red bill. Found in pairs or in small flocks in well-vegetated water bodies. Feeds on insects, molluscs and aquatic vegetation. The male displays to the female during the breeding season (June to September) by holding waterweeds in his bill and bowing to her with loud chuckles. The nest is a large pad of water plants made on floating vegetation.

White-breasted Waterhen *Amaurornis phoenicurus*
Local name: Tellabora netikodi (Telugu), Dauk (Hindi) Size : 32 cm.

This stocky, but smart-looking, rail has a white face and underparts, grey upper parts and rufous lower belly and vent. The stumpy tail is jerked up and down as the bird hunts for its prey (insects, worms, paddy shoots, marsh plants, etc.). It is silent except in the breeding season (coinciding with the monsoon) when it becomes exceedingly loud and noisy – sometimes calling through the night. Frequents water bodies (ponds, ditches, paddy fields, etc.) surrounded by thick vegetation, which offer it nesting space. The nest is located on the ground close to the water's edge.

Bronze-winged Jacana
Metapodius indicus
Local name: Kanchurekkala jacana (Telugu), Jal pipi (Hindi)
Size : 28 - 31 cm.

This long-legged, pigeon-sized water bird has a black head, black neck, black under parts, white eyebrow streak, bronze upper parts, rufous rump and enormous toes. It is usually found on floating vegetation in ponds and other water bodies. The wide spreading toes distribute its weight while walking on the water plants and prevent it from sinking. It is also a good swimmer. Seeds, roots of water plants, insects and other small aquatic animals are its food. The nesting season is between June and September. The nest is a pad of weeds made on floating vegetation.

Pheasant-tailed Jacana
Hydrophasianus chirurgus
Local name: Jamudutoke jacana, Neeti nemali (Telugu), Piho (Hindi)
Size : 31 cm.

This bird is pale brown and white in the non-breeding season. In the breeding season, it sports a bright white and chocolate brown plumage and an elongated sickle shaped tail (giving its Telugu name "*Neeti Nemali*" or water peacock). It is usually found in well-vegetated water bodies. The wide spreading toes distribute its weight while walking on water plants and prevent it from sinking. It is also a good swimmer. Seeds, roots of water plants, insects and other small aquatic animals are its food. The nesting season is between June and September. The nest is a pad of weeds made on floating vegetation. Sometimes eggs are laid directly on floating singara (water chestnut, *Trapa* sp.).

Little Ringed Plover
Charadrius dubius
Local name: Baitu ullanki (Telugu), Merwa (Hindi) Size : 14 - 17 cm.

This is a plump little wader with a prominent breast band, yellow eye-ring and white hind neck collar. Usually found in pairs or small parties on the banks of water bodies. Runs about in short spurts on the bank, pausing in between to pick up small invertebrates (insects and tiny crabs). The call is a clear descending "*pee-oo*" or a shorter "*peeu*". The nesting season is between March and August, though it varies locally. The nest is a small, unlined hollow on shingle on the water bank or among sparse vegetation.

Yellow-wattled Lapwing *Vanellus malabaricus*
Local name: Chiluva (Telugu), Zirdi (Hindi) Size : 26 - 28 cm.

A light brown bird with a white belly, prominent lobe shaped yellow wattles on its beak, long yellow legs and black cap. Usually seen in pairs or in small groups of about 4-5 birds in dry open country. The call is a frequently repeated rather plaintive "*chee-eet*" and a high-pitched "*twit-twit-twit-twit*". The nesting season is between April and July. The eggs are laid on bare ground in dry wasteland in a scrape that is sometimes lined with pebbles or goat/ sheep droppings.

Red-wattled Lapwing
Vanellus indicus
Local name: Yenappa chiluva (Telugu), Titori (Hindi)
Size : 32 - 35 cm.

This bird is likely to be encountered on grassy open spaces near water, usually in pairs. On closer approach it rises up giving its "*did-he-do-it?*" calls. The Red-wattled Lapwing gets its name from the red wattle (bare skin) in front of its eye. It feeds on insects, grubs, molluscs, etc. The nesting season is chiefly between March and August. The eggs are laid on bare ground and are cryptic in colouration, thus perfectly camouflaged.

Common Snipe *Gallinago gallinago*
Local name: Ullamu kuruvi (Telugu), Chaha (Hindi) Size : 25 - 27 cm.

This winter visitor has dark brown upper parts streaked with black, rufous and buff, and whitish under parts. It is a skulker and is usually found singly and occasionally in flocks at marshes, flooded paddy fields, and muddy edges of rivers and pools. It is usually active at night and in the early mornings and late evenings. When disturbed, it flies off abruptly with a rapid zigzag flight. The food of this bird consists of worms, insect larvae, etc., which it obtains from the soft mud by probing with its slender 5 cm long bill.

Common Redshank *Tringa totanus*
Local name: Yerrakalla Ullanki (Telugu), Chhota batan (Hindi). Size : 27 - 29 cm.

This wader is a winter visitor to our state. It is greyish brown above, white with fine brown streaks below and has red legs. In flight, a broad, white trailing edge to the wing is prominently seen. Found either singly or in small flocks at marshes, muddy edges of water bodies, tidal creeks and estuaries, etc. The call is a shrill piping "*tiwee-tiwee-tiwee*" or "*tiu-tiu-tiu*". It feeds by walking briskly or wading, picking its food from the surface or probing into the mud for it.

Little Stint *Calidris minuta*
Local name: Chinna ullanki (Telugu), Chhota pankowwa (Hindi) Size : 13 - 15 cm.

This tiny wader is grey-brown above, white below with black legs. A winter visitor, it is found in flocks near mudflats, coastal lagoons, tidal creeks, marshes, paddy fields and lakes. It is an active feeder, rapidly picking at the surface or darting about in search of prey. When disturbed, the whole flock takes off, twisting and turning in unison. The call, a weak *pi-pi-pi* is usually heard when the birds are in flight.

Common Sandpiper *Actitis hypoleucos*
Local name: Ullanki (Telugu), Titvari (Hindi) Size : 19 - 21 cm.

This small sandpiper has olive-brown upper parts and whitish under parts. It constantly bobs its tail up and down while feeding, often dunking and raising its head simultaneously. It is a winter visitor and stragglers may be found singly in the summer months near tanks, banks of streams and canals, coastal wetlands and rocky coasts. It runs along the water's edge picking up prey insects, worms, molluscs, etc., from the ground or vegetation. The flight is low over the water with rapid wing beats alternating with brief glides. The call is a *wee-wee-wee*, usually heard when the bird is alarmed.

Wood Sandpiper *Tringa glareola*
Local name: Podala ullanki (Telugu), Chupka (Hindi).
Size : 18 - 21 cm.

This widespread winter visitor has a prominent white eyebrow and yellowish legs. A sepia-brown body with heavily spotted upper parts, pale underside, white rump and back camouflage it well. It is found singly or in small flocks near well-vegetated shallow water such as marshes, edges of tanks and lakes, wet paddy, etc. It feeds by probing, picking prey (insects, larvae, worms and molluscs) from the surface and sweeping its bill from side to side in water. The feeding is accompanied by wagging the tail end of the body up and down. The call is a shrill *chiff-chiff-chiff* uttered when the bird is disturbed and takes off.

Stone Curlew *Burhinus oedicnemus*
Local name: Raati kaledu (Telugu), Bada Gulinda, Goar (Hindi).
Size: 40-44 cm.

This is a sandy brown bird, strongly streaked with dark brown, with a large yellow eye, short yellow-based black bill, and long yellow legs. Usually found in pairs or small groups in open dry and shrub country, resting by the day in the shade. When alarmed or suspicious, it takes off with a short sprint and then squats flat on the ground with its head on the ground, relying on camouflage to keep it safe. Feeds mainly on ground insects (beetles, grasshoppers, and termites), worms, small reptiles and mice. The nesting season is between February and August. The nest is a small scrape on the ground.

Black-winged Stilt
Himantopus himantopus
Local name: Nallarekkala Ullankipitta (Telugu), Gaz paon (Hindi) Size : 35 - 40 cm.

This bird is usually found in flocks in marshes, ponds and lakes. Its long legs help it to venture further into the water than most other waders. It is a lanky, white bird with black wings, a straight, long, black beak and thin, long, red legs. During the breeding season, the male sports a black cap. It picks up prey from the water surface and also probes in soft mud for worms, molluscs and aquatic insects while sweeping the bill from side to side. This wader is also a good swimmer. In flight the neck is extended in front while the long red legs trail behind. The call is a *kek-kek-kek* uttered when the bird takes flight when alarmed. The nesting season is between April and August. The nest is a depression in the ground lined with bits of vegetation.

Small Pratincole
Glareola lactea
Local name: Chinna lolapakshi (Telugu)
Size : 16 - 19 cm.

This is a small, dainty bird with pale sandy-grey colouration. In flight the wings show striking grey, black and white colours. It is usually found in small flocks on sandy and shingle-covered banks of large rivers and lakes. The calls include "*tuck-tuck-tuck*" and "*tiririt, tiririt, tiririt*". This bird is most active during the early mornings and late evenings and rests during the hot part of the day, squatting on the ground. It hawks insects (moths, beetles and flying ants) while in flight and also hunts for insects on the ground in a typical plover style. The breeding season is between February and April. The nest is a shallow scrape on a river sandbank or on rocky/sandy ground on a reservoir island.

Black-headed Gull *Larus ridibundus*
Local name: Nallatala gourukaki (Telugu), Dhomra (Hindi) Size : 38 cm.

This is a winter visitor to the coast and inland and is frequently spotted near harbours, fishing villages, large rivers and inland lakes. Grey above, white below, greyish-white head that turns a dark coffee colour by March. The wing has a pure white leading edge.The call is described as a loud scream "*ree-ah*" or a loud "*ka-yek, ka-yek*".

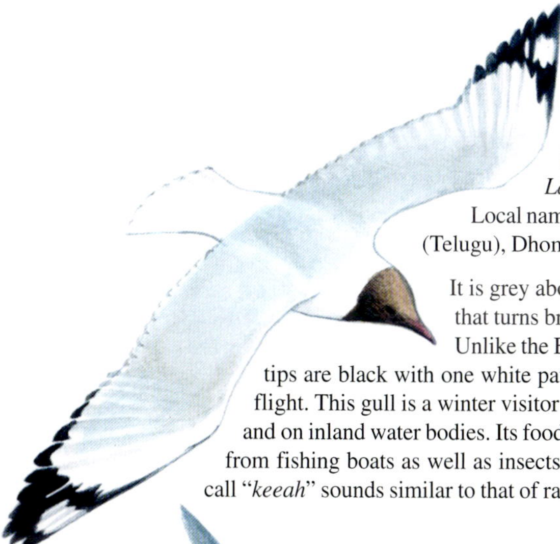

Brown-headed Gull
Larus brunnicephalus
Local name: Goodumatala gourukaki (Telugu), Dhomra (Hindi) Size : 42 cm.

It is grey above, white below, with a grey head that turns brown as the summer season begins. Unlike the Black-headed Gull, this bird's wing tips are black with one white patch in the centre, clearly visible in flight. This gull is a winter visitor and can be spotted along the coast and on inland water bodies. Its food includes scraps thrown overboard from fishing boats as well as insects, slugs and vegetation shoots. The call "*keeah*" sounds similar to that of raven. It breeds in Ladaka and Tibet.

Indian River Tern *Sterna aurantia*
Local name: Ramadasu (Telugu), Ganga cheel (Hindi) Size : 38 - 46 cm.

This is a smart grey-white bird with a forked tail, orange-yellow bill, black cap and nape, and red legs and feet. It is frequently seen at large rivers, lakes and tanks. It flies over the water, occasionally diving or picking up food (fish, shrimp, tadpoles and water insects) from the surface. The call is a high-pitched *kiuk-kiuk*. The nesting season is between November and August. The nest is made on bare sand on spits and islets in water bodies in a colony shared with the Indian Skimmer, Little Tern and Small Pratincole.

Yellow-legged Green-pigeon
Treron phoenicopterus
Local name: Pachcha guvva (Telugu), Harial (Hindi) Size : 33 cm.

This is a yellow, olive-green and ashy grey pigeon, found in small flocks in well-wooded country. It frequents large fruit trees such as banyan and peepul to feed on fruit and berries. Its call is a pleasant whistle. A favourite of the amateur hunter, its populations in the vicinities of cities have suffered considerably at their hands. The nesting season is mainly between March and June. The nest is a platform of twigs placed in a tree.

Blue Rock Pigeon *Columba livia*
Local name: Gaddi pauramu (Telugu), Kabootar (Hindi) Size : 33 cm.

This is a common bird in villages, towns and cities, where large numbers may be seen perched equidistant from each other on rooftops, beams and road lamps. It is a favourite of bird-fanciers and so several hybrids are often seen in parts of inhabited areas. Its food comprises of cereals and pulses. The call is a deep "*gootr-goo, gootr-goo*". Nesting is throughout the year and the nest is a collection of twigs placed on a ledge.

Emerald Dove *Chalcophaps indica*
Local name: Andibellaguvva (Telugu).
Size : 27 cm.

Stout, broad winged dove with a brown body, glistening emerald bronze-green wings and upperparts. Male has a grey head. Found singly or in pairs in the forest. Feeds on seeds and fallen berries pecking them off the ground. The call is a deep, mournful *tk-hoon...tk-hoon*. The nesting season is between January and May. The nest is a twig platform placed in a small tree, shrub or bamboo clump.

Eurasian Collared-Dove *Streptopelia decaocto*
Local name: Peddabella guvva (Telugu), Dhor fakta (Hindi) Size : 32 cm.

The black half-collar of this sandy-brown bird gives it the name ring dove. It is fairly common in open dry country and lightly wooded areas. It is rarely seen in gardens and about human habitations. The call of this bird is a deep and loud cooing "*kukkoo-kook*". There is no marked nesting season. The nest is a platform of twigs in a small tree.

Spotted Dove
Streptopelia chinensis
Local name: Chukkala guvva (Telugu), Chitta fakhta, Parki (Hindi)
Size : 30 cm.

The white spotted upper parts and the black-and-white chessboard pattern on the hind neck easily distinguish this dove. It is commonly found in urban gardens, fields and light forests. The call is a soft mournful "*krookruk-krukroo...kroo-kroo-kroo*". It is a ground-feeder, picking up grains, weed-seeds, etc. There is no definite nesting season. The nest is built fairly low in a tree, thorn bush, bamboo clump or palm.

Little Brown Dove
Streptopelia senegalensis
Local name: Sovata guvva (Telugu), Chota fakta (Hindi) Size : 27 cm.

This small, earth-brown dove is fairly common in dry open scrub country and in human habitations. Its food consists of seeds and grains, which is pecked from the ground. The call of the little brown dove is a soft, pleasant "*coo-rooroo-rooroo*". There is no clearly marked nesting season. The nest is a platform of twigs in a Euphorbia clump or in the rafters of old buildings.

Rose-ringed Parakeet *Psittacula krameri*
Local name: Rama chiluka (Telugu), Tota (Hindi). Size : 42 cm.

This is a green parakeet with a bright red bill. The male has a thin black collar. This common parakeet is usually found in the vicinity of human habitation and around cultivated lands. It is a pest in orchards where it feeds on fruit – wasting a lot more than it actually eats. It roosts communally in large trees. The call is a loud, shrill "*kee-ah*". Its breeding season is generally between December and July. The nest is made in a hole in a tree trunk, wall or cliff.

Plum-headed Parakeet *Psittacula cyanocephala*
Local name: Chiluka (Telugu), Tuiya tota (Hindi) Size : 36 cm.

This delicate parakeet is smaller in size than the Rose-ringed Parakeet and has a white-tipped long tail. The male has a bluish-red head and maroon shoulder-patches. The female has a violet-grey head, bright yellow collar round the neck and no maroon on her shoulders. It is usually found in wooded country and in the vicinity of forests. It roosts communally in large numbers in bamboo clumps or in other forest trees. The call is a shrill "*tooi?*" or "*tooi-tooi?*" The nesting season is primarily between January and May. The nest is a hole in a tree trunk, usually excavated by the birds.

White-breasted Kingfisher
Halcyon smyrnensis
local name: Tellaguntu buchchigaadu (Telugu), Kilkila (Hindi) Size : 28 cm.

This bird is quite at home even away from water and can be spotted perched on telephone wires along the roadside. It has chocolate-brown and turquoise blue feathers, and a bright white throat and chest patch. The call is described as a loud rattling laugh. The song is a chattering "*kililili*" – that gives it the Hindi name "*Kilkila*". The nesting season is between January and August. The nest is a horizontal tunnel dug in the mud-bank of a stream or earth-cutting.

Lesser Pied Kingfisher *Ceryle rudis*
Local name: Neela buchchigaadu (Telugu), Kilkila (Hindi) Size : 31 cm.

A black and white kingfisher. The female has a single broken breast band as compared to the double, complete breast band of the male. Usually found in large ponds and lakes, frequently hovering above the water at a height of about 10 metres or so, and making occasional dives to catch fish, tadpoles, frogs and aquatic insects. The call is a sharp "*chirruk, chirruk*". The nesting season is between October and May. The nest is a horizontal tunnel dug in the mud-bank of a stream.

Small Blue Kingfisher *Alcedo atthis*
Local name: Chinna neela buchchigaadu (Telugu), Chhota kilkila, Nita (Hindi) Size : 16 cm.

A smart blue and orange small kingfisher that is not very common to come by. It is usually seen perched on a small post or low branch beside water. It keeps an eye on the water for small fish, tadpoles and water insects from this perch. When spotted, the kingfisher makes a quick dive, captures the prey in its stout beak and returns to the perch to swallow the catch as a whole. Frequently flies low over water, from one perch to another, calling. The call is a high-pitched "*chee-chee*". The nesting season is between March and June. The nest is a horizontal tunnel dug in the mud-bank of a stream.

Asian Koel *Eudynamys scolopacea*
Local name: Kovila (Telugu), Koel (Hindi) Size : 43 cm.

The "*kuoo-kuoo*" call of this bird is the most familiar of summer sounds. The glistening black male with red eyes is the one who calls out. The dull coloured, spotted female gives out a sharp "*kik-kik-kik-kik*". This bird is often overlooked during the rest of the year owing to its silence during those months. It spends most of its time in the dense foliage of trees. Its food includes fruits (mainly figs), insects and birds' eggs. The koel is a brood parasite – laying its eggs in the nest of the house or jungle crow. The nesting season is between April and August to coincide with that of the host.

Small Green-billed Malkoha
Phaenicophaeus viridirostris
Local name: Pachchamukku vamanakaki (Telugu), Kappara, Popiya (Hindi) Size : 39cm.

The green bill, naked blue patch around the eye and long white-tipped tail make this green-grey coloured non-parasitic cuckoo an interesting sight. Usually found singly or in pairs in dry thorn jungle or in small trees along village roads. Rarely descends to the ground. The food of this bird includes caterpillars, large insects, lizards and other small animals. The nesting season is between March and May. The nest is an untidy twig platform placed in a euphorbia bush, bamboo clump, lantana shrubbery, etc.

Greater Coucal *Centropus sinensis*
Local name: Pedda jamudu kaki (Telugu), Mahoka (Hindi) Size : 48 cm.

This bird is often the first one to be 'spotted' and reported to budding birdwatchers by curious friends and family. It resembles the common crow but has a longer, broader tail and bright rust coloured wings. It spends most of its time on the ground pursuing prey – young birds, bird's eggs, insects, lizards, etc. The "*hoop...oop...oop...*" call of the Coucal is often heard in the city and a "conversation" is frequently held between two birds. The nesting season of the Coucal is between February and September. The nest is a globular mass of twigs, leaves, etc., close to the ground in a shrub.

Indian Plaintive Cuckoo

Cacomantis passerinus
Local name: Chinna katte pitta (Telugu)
Size : 34 cm.

This small and slender cuckoo is about the size of a red-vented bulbul with a longer tail. The female sometimes has a 'hepatic' or red-colour phase. Otherwise it resembles the male, which is a grey bird with white at the vent and under tail coverts. Usually found in lightly wooded country and prefers the tops of trees and bushes. Caterpillars and insects form its main diet. The call is a clear "*pee-pieu*" ascending in scale and pitch with every repetition. The breeding season is between July and October. The eggs are laid in the nests of small warblers such as the tailor-bird and ashy prinia. When hatched the young bird instinctively pushes the eggs of the host out of the nest securing for itself undivided attention and food from the parents.

Pied Crested Cuckoo

Clamator jacobinus
Local name: Golakokila (Telugu), Kokila, Chatak (Hindi) Size : 33 cm.

This attractive crested bird is strikingly black above and white below. White on the tips of the tail feathers and round patches on the wings, visible in flight. Frequents wooded places. It is considered the harbinger of the monsoon (*chataka pakshi*) probably because its migration into India coincides with the onset of the monsoon. The excited "*pi-piu*" call of this bird is commonly heard in May and June. Grasshoppers, caterpillars and wild berries are the chief food of this bird. The nesting season is between June and August. Eggs are laid in the nests of babblers.

Common Hawk Cuckoo *Hierococcyx varius*

Local name: Chinna katti pitta (Telugu) Size : 23 cm.

This bird resembles the Shikra in its plumage, flight and movements. It frequents groves, well-wooded campuses and light forests. The bird is silent in winter. With the advance of summer it makes its presence felt with its loud call – "*brain-fever, brain-fever*". This call is repeated on an ascending scale about half-a-dozen times before it suddenly stops and begins again a little later. The call gives the bird its other common name – the brain-fever bird. Food includes caterpillars, insects, berries and wild figs. Breeding is between March and June. This bird is parasitic and lays its eggs in a babbler's nest.

Asian Palm Swift *Cypsiurus balasiensis*
Local name: Tadi ababeel (Hindi), Telugu name not known. Size : 13 cm.

A dark grey bird with long, slender wings and deeply forked tail, like a small bow and arrow. Frequently found flying in groups in open country with palmyra palms, hawking tiny insects. Roosts and nests in the palmyra palm. Call is a shrill *ti-ti-tee*. Nesting season is throughout the year. The nest is a cup made of feathers and fibres, cemented with the bird's saliva onto the underside of a palm leaf.

House Swift *Apus affinis*
Local name:Ababeel (Hindi), Telugu name not known.
Size : 15 cm.

This is a smoky black bird with a white throat and rump. It is frequently found in the vicinity of old buildings, forts and large bridges – flying incessantly. Tiny insects are caught in its open beak in mid-flight. As all their four toes point forward (unlike most other perching birds where one toe points backwards), swifts cannot perch on branches like other birds do. Instead, they cling to rough surfaces such as old walls. The call is a rapid and shrill *siksiksiksik-sik-sik-siksiksiksik*. The nesting season is chiefly between February and September. The nest is a cup of feathers and straw cemented with the birds' saliva to a wall. It is a colonial nester.

Common Indian Nightjar *Caprimulgus asiaticus*
Local name: Bharata reyipitta (Telugu), Chapka (Hindi) Size : 24 cm.

This nocturnal bird is a dull grey-brown in colour, mottled and streaked – designed to merge perfectly with its surroundings where it spends the day crouching on the ground under the shelter of a low bush or on a low branch. It is active towards the late evening and through the night when it hawks moths and beetles and other insects in the air. This bird usually inhabits thinly wooded scrub country, fallow cultivation, young plantations, boulder-strewn country-side, etc. The call is a haunting "*chuk-chuk-chuk-chuk-r-r-r*". The nesting season is between February and September. The eggs are laid on bare ground under bushes.

Eurasian Eagle Owl *Bubo bubo*
Local name: Yerra gudlagooba (Telugu), Ghughu (Hindi)
Size : 55 - 66 cm.

This owl has upright ear tufts or 'horns'. It is a tawny, mottled owl with heavily streaked underparts.This nocturnal bird is found in wooded areas, scrub-covered hills, rocky outcrops, ruined forts, etc. It spends the day roosting under a bush or a rocky projection or in large trees. The call is a penetrating *tu-whooh*, the second note rising in tone. It feeds on small mammals, birds, reptiles, large insects, fish and crabs. The nesting season is between October and May. Eggs are laid on bare soil on a ledge, under a bush or in a natural depression.

Barn Owl *Tyto alba*
Local name: Chavu pitta (Telugu), Karail (Hindi). Size : 36 cm.
This owl has a white, heart-shaped face, pale under parts and golden-buff and grey upper parts. It is commonly found in and around human habitation – deserted buildings, tree holes, groves, etc. It roosts by day and is active in the late evening and night to hunt for rats and mice. The barn owl makes a variety of eerie screeching and hissing noises. The nesting season is spread throughout the year and the nest is a collection of straw, twigs, rags and rubbish within a tree hollow or a building.

Spotted Owlet *Athene brama*
Local name: Pagati kante (Telugu), Oolloo (Hindi). Size : 21 cm.

This common little owl is greyish-brown, spotted with white, with a large head and staring yellow eyes. It is usually found in villages, towns, cities, ruins, cultivated lands, groves, etc. It roosts during the day in a tree hollow, shady branch or under roofs. When disturbed, it stares at the intruder, comically bobbing its head up and down. The call is a harsh "*chirrur-chirrur-chirrur*" or "*chevak-cheevak-cheevak*". Its food comprises of beetles, other insects, young birds, mice and lizards. The nesting season is generally between November and April, but may vary locally. The nest is placed in a hole in a tree or wall.

Blue-tailed Bee-eater *Merops philippinus*
Local name: Kommu passirika (Telugu), Bada patringa (Hindi) Size : 23 - 26 cm.

This bird resembles the Green Bee-eater and is a winter migrant to our area. However, it can be distinguished by its larger size, the black stripe running through the eye and the absence of the black necklace. It prefers areas that are well wooded and those that are near streams or open water. The food and feeding habits are similar to those of the Green Bee-eater. The nesting season is between March and June. The nest is an excavated tunnel in a river-bank usually in the company of several such others.

Green Bee-eater *Merops orientalis*
Local name: Chinna pasirika (Telugu), Patringa, Harrial (Hindi) Size : 16 - 18 cm.

The fine green colour, rust brown head, black stripe through the eye, sharp beak, a black necklace and the 'wire' in the tail make this bird unmistakable. From its perch on a telephone wire or post, the bird takes off expertly after flying insects (bees, wasps, dragonflies, termites, etc.). It returns to its perch with its catch, and if too large, batters the prey to death before swallowing it. Green Bee-eaters gather in large numbers for roosting. Several dozens may be found sitting huddled together, on a wire. The nesting season is generally between March and June. The nest is a horizontal tunnel, about half a metre to two metres long, in a mud bank ending with a wide egg-chamber.

Indian Roller *Coracias benghalensis*
Local name: Pala pitta (Telugu) Size : 33 cm.

This stocky bird flashes its brilliantly coloured wings in flight, displaying light and dark blue bands. It has a big head, heavy bill, rufous chest and a pale blue abdomen. It is frequently seen perched on telephone wires over farmlands on the lookout for insects, frogs and lizards. Call is a croaky *chack-chak-chak*, also with various screeches and shrieks. The nesting season is between March and July. The nest is a collection of grass, bits of paper and rags in a tree-hollow or in a hole in a building wall. It is the state bird of Andhra Pradesh and is considered a friend of the farmer, as it preys on insects in agricultural fields.

Common Hoopoe *Upupa epops*
Local name: Kukudu pitta (Telugu), Hudhud (Hindi) Size : 31 cm.

A pale brown-coloured bird with a prominent fan-shaped crest and black-and-white zebra markings on the wings and tail. It is usually spotted on grass lawns and on the ground in light wooded areas, probing for insects, bugs, etc., with its long and slightly curved beak. The crest is fanned out from time to time. The call is a monotonous "*hoop-hoop, hoop-hoop*". The flight path of the hoopoe is undulating. The nesting season is between February and May. The nest is a hollow in a tree or a hole in a wall lined with rags and rubbish. It is an untidy nest-keeper and the nest is infamous for the stench it emits.

Indian Grey Hornbill ***Ocyceros birostris***

Local name: Kommu kasiri (Telugu), Dhanmar (Hindi) Size : 50 cm.

A shaggy-looking grey bird, larger than the Jungle Crow. The huge black and white c bill with a 'casque' attached to it and the seemingly loosely attached tail gives it a co look. Frequently spotted in huge banyan and other fig trees when they are in fruit. animals, insects and lizards also form a part of its diet. The commonly used call is a shriek, "*chee-ooww*". It flies with a few rapid and noisy wing strokes followed by a di glide, typical of all hornbills. The nesting season is between March and June. The nest hornbill is well known for its uniqueness. The female is sealed off in the tree-hollow nest a wall made of the birds' own droppings, except for a narrow window to receive food fro male. Once the eggs hatch the female breaks the wall and comes out. The wall is replaste keep the hatchlings safe. Both parents now feed the growing chicks until they are large eno come out of this nursery.

Coppersmith Barbet
Megalaima haemacephala
Local name: Kamsali pitta (Telugu), Chota basanth (Hindi)
Size : 17 cm.

This bird is about the size of a sparrow but is more heavily built. The grass green body, crimson neck and forehead, and yellow throat make it a rather colourful bird – yet it is more commonly heard than seen. The call, a loud, metallic, monotonous "*tonk, tonk, tonk*", is commonly heard in the vicinity of large fruit trees, especially fig trees. In addition to fruits and berries, insects sometimes form part of its diet. The nesting season is between January and June. The nest is a hole the bird digs out in the dead branch of a softwood tree such as Coral or Drumstick.

Large Green Barbet
Megalaima zeylanica
Local name: Godumatala kamsalipitta (Telugu), Bada basanta (Hindi)
Size : 27 cm.

A heavy billed, grass-green bird with a bare orange patch around the eye. Its face, breast and abdomen are streaked with brown and white. Found singly or in small groups in fruiting trees, usually in company of other fruit-eating birds in large fig trees. Very noisy in summer when its monotonous *kutroo, kutroo, kutroo* or *kutruk, kutruk, kutruk* call can be heard from afar. The breeding season is between February and October. The nest is a hole excavated in a rotten branch.

Lesser Golden-backed Woodpecker
Dinopium benghalense
Local name: Vadarangipitta (Telugu), Katphora (Hindi) Size : 26 - 29 cm.

This attractive bird is usually seen in lightly wooded places, trees around cultivation and large gardens. Its upper plume is golden - yellow and black. Male has a crimson forehead and crest. Female has a crimson crest, but spotted black forehead. Its breast is buffy-white, streaked with black. Found climbing up trees or branches, straight up or by going around in a spiral. Taps away rotten wood to catch grubs and insects underneath. Sometimes hunts black ants on the ground. It also eats ripe fruit and nectar. The call is a loud laugh – *kyi-kyi-kyi*. Flight is dipping – typical of woodpeckers. The nesting season is throughout the year. The nest is a hollow in a tree trunk or branch, dug out by the birds.

Brown-capped Pygmy Woodpecker
Dendrocopos nanus
Local name: Chitta surutipakshi (Telugu), Katphora (Hindi)
Size : 13 cm.

This small woodpecker is dark brown above and dull white below with faint brown streaks on the belly. A broad white stripe runs from its eye down to the side of the neck and white spots on central tail feathers. Male has a narrow scarlet streak on either side of the head. Found singly or in pairs in light deciduous forests or in trees near cultivation. Frequents slender branches of tall trees and saplings. Feeds on insects, flower-nectar, figs, berries, etc. Call is a metallic *tik-ik-ik-ik-r-r-r*. Nesting season is between February and April. The nest is a hollow in a rotten branch or a hole dug out by the birds.

Rufous-tailed Finch-Lark

Ammomanes phoenicurus
Local name: Ambati jorigadu (Telugu)
Size : 16 cm.

A squat, dark rufous-brown lark with a rufous tail ending in a black band. Found in pairs or small flocks in dry open country, ploughed fields, fallow land, etc. Usually found on the ground, running about in a zigzag fashion, picking up grass and weed seeds, grains and small insects. Disturbs small insects out of their hiding places in the soil by rapid flicking of its wings. The display of the male during the breeding season is similar to that of the Ashy-crowned Finch-lark. The nesting season is between February and May. The nest is a cup of grasses made in a slight depression in the ground.

Ashy-crowned Sparrow-lark

Eremopterix grisea
Local name: Potti pichika (Telugu), Diyora, deoli (Hindi) Size : 12 cms.

A small, squat sparrow-like grey bird with a prominent black belly in males. Usually encountered as a pair, sitting in the midst of a dusty track or path, rising up only on close approach. The female looks like a smaller version of the sparrow.The flight display of the male is a treat to watch. He rises up in the air and then dives vertically downwards. This performance is repeated several times to the accompaniment of a long thin whistle. This bird feeds on seeds and tiny insects. The nesting season is throughout the year. The nest is a small depression in the ground, lined with grasses and rimmed with small stones – usually under the shelter of a stone or tiny bush.

Red-winged Bushlark

Mirafra erythroptera
Local name: Chinna eelajitha (Telugu), Aggiya (Hindi). Size : 14 cms.

A dull-coloured bird, with a large chestnut patch on the wings, conspicuous in flight. Frequents dry open country. The call is a "*tit-tit-tit*" followed by long, drawn-out whistles "*tsweeeih-tsweeeih-tsweeeih*". The male displays throughout the day in the breeding season (between March and October). Beginning his song flight from the top of a bush or post, he flies upwards with rapid wing beats, and parachutes down with the wings held motionless and raised in a wide V. The nest is a well-concealed shallow cup or dome of grass, placed in a small depression or at the base of a bush or stone.

Dusky Crag-Martin

Hirundo concolor

Local name: Dummurangu kondavana koyila (Telugu), Chatan ababil (Hindi)

Size : 13 cm.

A dark brown bird with a short, square tail and swallow-like wings. A white spot is clearly seen on all tail feathers except the middle and outermost ones, in flight. Found usually in deserted buildings, cliffs, caves, etc., in the company of swallows and swifts. It captures insects in mid-air. Call is a soft "*chit-chit*" uttered in flight. The nesting season is between June and October. The nest is a deep half-cup of mud, lined with feathers and reinforced with plant stems, attached to a rock face or wall under an overhanging rock or roof.

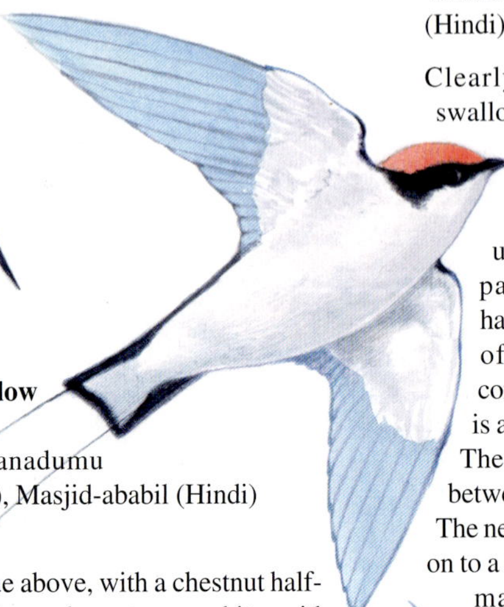

Red-rumped Swallow

Hirundo daurica

Local name: Yerranadumu vanakoyila (Telugu), Masjid-ababil (Hindi)

Size : 16 - 17 cm.

This bird is steel blue above, with a chestnut half-collar and rump. The underparts are white, with brown streaks. Usually seen as a pair or in small parties hunting insects in mid-air. In winter (when numbers are increased by migratory races that fly in) large parties gather in communal roosts or on telephone wires. Nesting is from April to August. The retort-shaped nest is made of mud, plastered to a wall and ceiling corner or overhanging rock surface. The hollow egg chamber is lined with feathers.

Common Swallow

Hirundo rustica

Local name: Vanakoyila (Telugu), Ababil (Hindi)

Size : 18 cm.

Glossy steel blue or deep purple above and pinkish-white below. With a deeply forked tail, chestnut forehead and throat. A black pectoral band lines the chestnut throat patch. Usually found in groups in open country or near water, sitting close together on telephone wires or hawking insects in the air, high up or close to the ground. This winter visitor roosts in large numbers in reed beds. Call is a clear *vit-vit*.

Wire-tailed Swallow

Hirundo smithii

Local name: Teegatoka vanakoyila (Telugu), Ababbil (Hindi) Size : 14 cm.

Clearly made out from other swallows by the two wire ends to the tail. Glossy steel blue above with a chestnut cap and glistening white underparts. Usually found in pairs or small groups, hawking insects in the vicinity of water bodies. Roosts communally in reed beds. Call is a *chirrik-weet* or a *chit-chit*. The nesting season is mainly between March and September. The nest is made of mud plastered on to a wall or rock surface to make a cup-like structure.

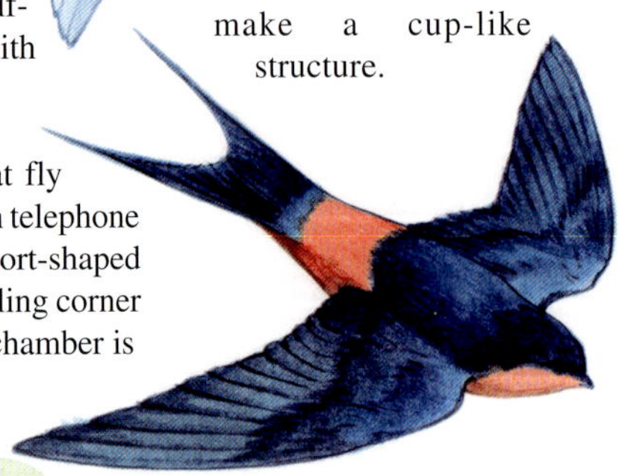

Grey Wagtail *Motacilla cinerea*
Local name: Tella kumpa jitta (Telugu), Dhoban (Hindi) Size : 19 cm.

A grey and yellow bird. In summer, the chin and throat turn black in males. This winter visitor is found near rocky streams. It runs briskly in spurts, wagging its tail and chasing tiny insects for food.The call is a sharp *stit* ot *zeefit* or *chicheep,chicheep*. It breeds in the Himalayas.

Large Pied Wagtail
Motacilla maderaspatensis
Local name: Sakala sarela-gadu (Telugu), Khanjan (Hindi)
Size : 21 cm.

As the name indicates, this wagtail is pied – a striking black and white bird with a white eyebrow on its black face. It is most likely to be encountered near water bodies, but can be sometimes spotted on housetops, calling melodiously. This is our only resident wagtail and so can be seen through the year. Usually found in pairs, it nests between March and October. The nest is a cup-shaped structure made of grass and rootlets, usually placed in a crevice or a hole located near water. It feeds on insects.

Paddyfield Pipit *Anthus rufulus*
Local name:Bharatha Jittangi , Gurapa-modi-pitta (Telugu), Charchari (Hindi) Size : 15 cm.

This is a dull, earth-coloured, slim bird that stands tall on thin legs and has a slender bill and long tail. It is found in pairs or in small parties in open areas, grasslands and ploughed fields running about on the ground in spurts and wagging its tail slowly up and down. When disturbed it flies away with an undulating flight and a "*pipit, pipit*" or "*tseep, tseep*" call. The nesting season is between February and October. The nest is a shallow cup of grass, rootlets and hair placed under the shelter of a clod of earth or in a dried-up hoof-print.

Ashy Swallow-Shrike *Artamus fuscus*
Local name: Tadi pitta (Telugu), Tadi ababeel (Hindi) Size : 19 cm.

This is a slaty grey bird with pinkish pale underparts, and a narrow whitish horseshoe shaped band across its upper tail coverts. Found in small parties, huddled together on telephone wires or on dead branches of tall trees and hawking insects (moths, butterflies and other flying insects) in flight. Inhabits open wooded country, often with palm trees. When sitting, the stumpy tail is constantly wagged up and down and sideways. It calls frequently in flight and when perched. In flight, it resembles a swallow.The call is a harsh *chek-chek-chek*. The nesting season is between January and July. The nest is a shallow cup made of fine fibres, grass and roots placed on a horizontal branch or at the base of a leaf stalk of a palm tree.

Small Minivet *Pericrocotus cinnamomeus*
Local name:Chinna kumkum pujitha (Telugu), Bulalchashm, Saheli (Hindi) Size : 16 cm.

A small, bright-coloured bird that keeps to the tops of trees in light forest. The male has a black head, grey upper parts, orange-yellow underparts. The female and juvenile are paler- grey and yellow. Usually found in small flocks, minivets fly from tree to tree, one after the other. Feeds on insects and larvae. The call is a far-carrying mousy squeak, "*swee-swee*". Nesting is from February to September. The nest is a shallow cup of fibres plastered with cobwebs attached to a high branch. "Aunts" assist a breeding pair raise their brood.

Scarlet Minivet *Pericrocotus flammeus*
Local name: Kumkum pujitha (Telugu), Pahari bulalchashm (Hindi) Size : 20-22 cm.

This forest bird is almost always spotted in small groups moving about in the canopy. It is often a member of mixed feeding-parties of birds. Males are black with scarlet underparts and wing bars. Females and juveniles are grey with olive-yellow underparts and wingbars.The call is a pleasant whistle, described as *whee-tweet*, *sweep, sweep* or *whiriri, whiriri*. The nesting season is between April and July. The nest is a neat cup of rootlets and fibres bound with cobwebs, placed on a horizontal branch.

Red-vented Bulbul *Pycnonotus cafer*
Local name: Pigili pitta (Telugu), Bulbul (Hindi)
Size : 20 cm.

This is one of the most familiar of our garden birds, found usually in pairs. It is a coffee- brown bird with a crested black head and bright under-tail coverts. A white rump-patch is conspicuous in flight. The bulbul's song is much like a melodious gurgle. It feeds on fruits (figs, lantana berries, etc.) and insects. It nests mostly between February and May. The nest is a compact cup of small twigs, stalks, etc., lined with fibres or fine rootlets, and bound together with cobwebs, placed in a bush.

White-browed Bulbul *Pycnonotus luteolus*
Local name: Pada pigili (Telugu), Khar bulbul (Hindi) Size : 20 cm.

This sober olive green-brown coloured bird has conspicuous white eyebrows and pale underparts. It typically inhabits shrubbery in open scrubland – though it also visits overgrown home gardens. Banyan and peepul figs, ber and lantana berries, insects and flower nectar comprise its food. It has a sharp staccato call. The nesting season is between March and September. The nest is a cup of small twigs and rootlets in a bush placed under 2 m from the ground.

Red-whiskered Bulbul *Pycnonotus jocosus*
Local name: Turaka pigili pitta (Telugu), Pahari bulbul (Hindi)
Size : 20 cm.

Found in well-wooded areas and in large gardens. Similar to the red-vented bulbul, but has a prominent red patch on the cheeks and under the tail. It has a black, upstanding crest. Often seen perching on the tops of bushes. Feeds on fruit, insects, buds and flower nectar. It has a joyous , musical call. The nesting season is between February and August. The nest is a cup of small twigs, rootlets, grass, etc. placed in a low bush or creeper.

Common Iora *Aegithina tiphia*

Local name: Pasapu jitha (Telugu), Shaubeegi (Hindi) Size : 14 cm.

The non-breeding male and the female look similar with yellowish green upper parts and green tail.The breeding male has black and yellowish green upper parts (depending on the race) and a black tail. Usually found in pairs on trees in urban gardens or in groves outside villages, one bird calling to the other. The call is a series of short "*chee-chit-chit-chit*" notes. The iora's song is like its Hindi name "*shaubeegi*" – it has also been described as "*wheee-teeooo*". The bird spends its time hopping from branch to branch in trees hunting for insects and caterpillars. The nesting season is between May and September. The shallow cup-shaped nest plastered with cobwebs is placed in the fork of a twig.

Rufous-backed Shrike

Lanius schach

Local name: Podugutoka bilinchi (Telugu), Kajala latora (Hindi) Size : 25 cm.

This shrike has a grey head, bright rufous rump and lower back and a black band across the eyes.It is easy to spot, as it perches on edges of bushes or on posts. Found singly in bushy or lightly wooded country. Noisy in the mornings and evenings, it is also a good mimic. Feeds on grasshoppers, large insects, lizards, etc. Nesting season is between February and July. The nest is a deep cup made of twigs, grass, wool, rags, etc. placed in the fork of a branch of a small tree.

Southern Grey Shrike

Lanius meridionalis

Local name: Pedda bilinchi (Telugu), Bada latora (Hindi) Size : 24 cm.

Larger than the rufous backed shrike, this silver-grey bird has a long black and white tail and a thick black band across its eyes. Generally found singly, perched on bushes or on a fencepost in open scrub country. Keeps a look out for prey such as lizards, small mice, and insects, from its perch. Prey is torn to pieces before being eaten. Sometimes surplus food is stored by impaling it on thorns – this habit gives it the name butcher-bird. This bird is a good mimic of other birds' calls. The nesting season is in the summer and the nest is a deep bulky cup made of thorny twigs lined with grass, feathers, etc usually in a babool tree or a thorny bush.

Blue Rock-Thrush *Monticola solitarius*
Local name: Neeligante pitta , Podakachi pitta (Telugu) Size : 20 cm.

The male is bright indigo-blue, the female is grey-brown above with brown and white cross bars below. This winter visitor is usually seen singly on rocky outcrops, boulder strewn hill slopes, ruins and sometimes around occupied dwellings. It perches upright on a rock, flitting its tail jerkily. It is territorial, returning to the same area every year. Feeds on insects which it picks off the ground. Also feeds on Banyan and Peepal figs, berries and small lizards. It breeds in the Himalayas from April to June.

Indian Robin *Saxicoloides fulicata*
Local name: Nallanchi (Telugu), Kalachuri (Hindi) Size : 19 cm.

The male is a smart looking black bird with a white shoulder patch and terracota red under the root of the tail. The female is dull brown and lacks the shoulder patch. Usually seen as a pair, in dry scrub country, perched on a rock or on a low bush. The tail is held cocked. Hops and runs about on open ground picking up insects and grubs. The nesting season is between April and June. The nest is a shallow cup of grass, rootlets and rubbish lined with feathers or hair, built within a discarded tin or pot, a hole in the wall or earth bank or in any convenient cavity.

Oriental Magpie-Robin *Copsychus saularis*
Local name: Pedda nallanchi (Telugu), Dhaiyal (Hindi) Size : 23 cm.

This bird is black/slaty grey and white, with white on wings and sides of the tail. This usually silent bird is generally noticed only in the breeding season when the male, one of our most accomplished urban songsters, sings a loud whistling song in the mornings and later afternoons. This bird is also a good mimic of other bird's calls. it hops about on the ground (on lawns and under trees) looking for insects. It also feeds on flower nectar. The breeding season is summer. The nest is made in a cavity (in an old wall, tree trunk, etc.) and is a pad of grass, rootlets, hair, etc.

Pied Bushchat *Saxicola caprata*
Local name: Kampa nallanchi (Telugu) Size : 13.5 cm.

The male is black with white patches on the rump, abdomen and wings. The wing patches are conspicuous in flight. The female is dull brown with a rust coloured patch on the rump. It usually inhabits open scrublands and can be seen perched on the top of a small bush from where it takes off on short flights pursuing insects in the air or on the ground. The nesting season is between February and May. The nest is a stout mass of grass with a neat, deep cup, lined with fine rootlets, built in a cavity in the ground or in a bank, under the shelter of grass or weeds.

Common Stonechat *Saxicola torquata*
Local name: Banda nallanchi (Telugu) Size : 17 cm.

The male has a black head, orange-brown chest and prominent white 'collar' patches on the sides of the neck and shoulders, and rump. The female is dull brown with dark streaks on the upper parts. It usually inhabits areas near cultivation and reedy marshes. It is a winter visitor in our area, from the Himalayas. It feeds on insects and keeps a look out for them from atop a bush or reed – constantly flicking its tail up and down.

Black Redstart *Phoenicurus ochruros*
Local name:Nune buddi gaadu (Telugu) Size : 15 cm.

This slim black bird is often seen singly in scrub country or in lightly wooded places. It often perches on rocks, low bushes, etc., frequently vibrating its orange-chestnut tail. Food consists of insects and spiders, often picked off the ground and sometimes caught mid-air. The redstart is a migrant and heralds the arrival of the cold weather in our country. The call is a sharp trill.

Bluethroat *Luscinia svecica*
Local name: Podala neelakandam (Telugu), Hussaini pidda (Hindi) Size : 15 cm.

This slim, robin-like, olive-brown bird is a winter visitor to our areas from the Himalaya, north Europe and north Asia. The upper parts are brown, there is a whitish eyebrow, the tail is a bright chestnut – visible in flight – bordered with black and the under parts are pale white. The male has a brilliant blue bib on its throat and chest, with a white or rufous patch in the middle. The Bluethroat is found generally in the vicinity of wetlands. It feeds on caterpillars, small beetles and other insects.

Jungle Babbler ***Turdoides striatus***
Local name: Adavi saidaapitta (Telugu), Sat bhai (Hindi) Size : 25 cm.

This bird is frequently encountered in groups of seven or more, hence the popular name "seven sisters" or "*saat bhai*" in Hindi. It is light brown in colour and rather untidy. Flocks hunt for insects amongst leaf litter in open jungle, well-wooded compounds, gardens and groves of trees. Birds hop amidst the litter, one hop at a time, overturn fallen leaves and search for insects. Figs, berries and nectar from flowers of the Coral, Silk Cotton and other trees also form part of their diet. The noisy, seemingly endless chatter they often indulge in gives this group of birds the name "babblers". Nesting can be at any time of the year. The nest is a cup built from twigs, rootlets and grass in the fork of a leafy branch and is generally 2 to 3 metres from the ground. Its nest is parasitised by cuckoos.

White-headed Babbler
Turdoides affinis
Local name: Verry chinda (Telugu)
Size : 23 cm.

This bird gets its name from its pale coloured crown. It has a musical call quite unlike that of its cousins. It is quite common in Hyderabad and is frequently seen in small flocks in home gardens as well as in open scrub. Insects, small animals and wild fruit form its diet. The nesting season is between January and November. The nest is a bowl of twigs and rootlets built in a low bush. It is parasitised by the cuckoo family.

Large Grey Babbler
Turdoides malcolmi
Local name: Pasapu mukku chittaruvi (Telugu), Ghogoi (Hindi) Size : 28 cm.

This is a pale grey-brown bird with a long graduated tail, the white outer feathers of which are visible when the tail is spread during flight. Usually found in groups of about a dozen or so in cultivated country dotted with trees. A noisy incessant "*kay-kay-kay*" call reveals its presence. Nesting can be at any time of the year. The nest is a cup built from twigs, rootlets and grass in the fork of a leafy branch and is generally at a height of less than 5 metres from the ground. Parasitised by members of the cuckoo family.

Yellow-eyed Babbler *Chrysomma sinense*
Local name: Yerra kali jitta (Telugu), Bulal chashm (Hindi) Size : 18 cm.

This bird is chestnut-brown above and white below, with a striking yellow ring around its red eye. Small flocks move about in dense shrubs and tall grass hunting for insects, and are hence not very easy to come across. Its far-carrying call, once learnt, is a dead give-away. Berries and flower nectar also form part of their food. The nesting season is in the monsoon (June to September). The nest is a deep neat cup of fibres cemented with cobwebs made within one metre from the ground, in bushes.

Tailor Bird *Orthotomus sutorius*
Local name: Likku jitha (Telugu), Phutki, Durzee (Hindi) Size : 13 cm.

A perky little garden bird, olive-green above and white below, with a cocked pointed tail. Flits from twig to twig, searching for insects. Call is a loud and clear *tuwit-tuwit*. The nesting season is between April and September. The nest is made of soft fibres and is placed in a purse made by the bird by stitching two leaves or folding over the sides of one leaf – not too high from the ground.

Ashy Prinia *Prinia socialis*
Local name: Boodi rangu kampajitha (Telugu), Kali Phutki (Hindi) Size : 13 cm.

The long, jauntily held tail, the ashy-grey upper parts, and the cream-coloured under parts make this bird easily identifiable. The ashy prinia is a frequent visitor to gardens, hunting for insects. Its call is a sharp "*tee-tee-tee*". At times, the bird also makes a crackling sound with its wings, as it suddenly takes off on short flight spurts. The nesting season is between March and September. The nest is either a funnel of stitched leaves or an oblong purse of woven fibres bound with cobwebs to leaves of a low bush.

Paradise Flycatcher *Terpsiphone paradisi*
Local name: Toka pigili pitta (Telugu), Sultan bulbul (Hindi) Size : 20 cm.

The adult male is a sight to behold – in brilliant white with long twin tail feathers trailing behind as he flies through the forest. The female and the younger male are chestnut brown. This bird is comfortable amidst trees – and is found in forests, orchards and well-wooded gardens. A harsh "*che-chew*" call is made in the breeding season (February to July). The nest is a woven cup of fine fibres and grasses, snuggly fitted into the fork of a small branch.

Tickell's Blue-Flycatcher *Cyornis tickelliae*
Local name: Tickell neeli eegapattu (Telugu) Size : 14 cm.

Its striking blue colour, orange breast, white belly and compact size make this bird an endearing sight. It is usually found in the undergrowth in dry forest, wooded gardens, etc., where it perches on a low twig or vine, flicking its tail from time to time. From this perch, it makes short sallies after flies and other insects that form its staple diet. The song is described as a metallic trill of six or ten notes, the first half descending and the second half ascending! The nesting season is between March and August. The nest is an untidy cup of twigs, rootlets and leaves placed in a tree-hollow, earth-bank or bamboo clump.

White-browed Fantail-Flycatcher *Rhipidura aureola*
Local name: Tella kanubommala dasaripitta (Telugu), Chakdil (Hindi) Size : 18 cm.

This sooty dark-brown bird has a white supercilium, dark ear-coverts, greyish-brown upper parts, white belly and a dark tail with white tips. It is commonly found in dry open forests, gardens, etc. and limits itself to the lower and middle storeys, taking off from its perch to make graceful looping flights in the air to capture flies and other insects. The song is described as an ascending and then descending series of whistles "*chee-chee-cheweechee-vi*". The nesting season is between February and August. The nest is a compact cup of fine grass and cobwebs placed in the fork of a low twig.

Purple Sunbird *Nectarinia asiatica*

Local name: Udatena pitta (Telugu), Phul sunghni (Hindi) Size: 10 cm.

This familiar garden bird may look dark, almost black from a distance, but a closer look in good sunlight reveals its iridescent plumage. This plumage belongs to the male in the breeding season. The female and the non-breeding male are a much duller olive brown above and pale yellow below. Sunbirds are nectar feeders, and their specially designed down-curved bill helps to probe into flowers and suck up the nectar with their tubular tongues. They also eat spiders, small insects, caterpillars, etc. The Purple Sunbird nests mostly between March and May. The nest is an oblong purse made of soft grasses, cobwebs, human hair, etc., with a porch over its entrance-hole, hanging from the end of a twig.

Purple-rumped Sunbird *Nectarinia zeylonica*

Local name: Mudaga jitha (Telugu), Shakarkhora (Hindi) Size : 10 cm.

These garden birds are usually spotted in pairs. It flits from plant to plant in search of nectar and small insects, calling *tityou, tityou, tityou* constantly. The male has metallic crimson, green and purple upperparts and yellow underparts.It nests throughout the year. The nest is an oblong purse made of soft grasses, cobwebs, human hair, etc. hanging from the end of a twig.

Tickell's Flowerpecker *Dicaeum erythrorhynchos*

Local name: Paalina mukku (Telugu), Phoolchuki (Hindi) Size : 8 cm.

A tiny olive-brown bird with whitish under parts and a short, flesh-coloured bill. Frequents urban gardens (especially the Singapore cherry tree), orchards and light forests – where it seeks tiny berries and small fruit. The berries of the plant parasites *Dendrophthoe* and *Viscum* are its staple diet. It swallows these whole and deposits the seeds on other branches through its droppings, helping these parasitic mistletoes to spread. This active bird constantly gives a sharp "*chik-chik-chik*" call as it moves about from branch to branch. The nesting season is from February to June. The hanging oblong purse-like nest is suspended from a twig about 3-12 metres from the ground.

Black-headed Bunting *Emberiza melanocephala*
Local name: Nallatala jinuvayi (Telugu), Gandam (Hindi) Size: 16-18 cm.

These are slender, sparrow-like yellow birds with noticeable forked tails. The male has black on the head and a chestnut mantle. The female is a duller version of the male with smooth, yellow-buff underparts.

Red-headed Bunting *Emberiza bruniceps*
Local name: Yerratala jinuvayi (Telugu), Gandam (Hindi) Size : 16 - 18 cm.

Smaller than the black headed bunting, this bunting has a shorter bill, reddish head and yellow-green mantle and unstreaked body.

The Red-headed and Black-headed Buntings are winter visitors that arrive in September/ October and depart in March/April. They can be spotted in large flocks on farmlands, especially where the fields are interspersed with thickets. They feed on cereal seeds. The call is a musical *tweet*.

Black-headed Munia ***Lonchura malacca***

Local name: Nalla jinuvayi (Telugu), Nakkalnor (Hindi) Size : 11.5 cm.

A small chestnut bird with a stout, pointed bill, black head, neck, vent and thighs, and a white belly. Found in flocks in marshes, grasslands, paddy cultivation, reed beds, etc. Feeds on grass and weed seeds. Nesting season is between June and October. The nest is a large ball of grass built in low bushes or amongst tall grass or sugarcane stems within two metres from the ground.

Spotted Munia ***Lonchura punctulata***

Local name: Chukkala jinuvayi (Telugu), Telia munia (Hindi)
Size : 10.5 - 12 cm.

This otherwise plain brown bird sports chocolate-brown upper parts and white under parts speckled with black. Found in small groups in the outskirts of towns, near cultivated fields, open country with bushes, gardens, etc. Feeds on small berries and seeds. Roots communally in sugarcane fields and lantana bushes. Also roosts in nests used in the earlier breeding seasons or in those built for the purpose of providing a roost. The nesting season is chiefly between July and October. The nest is a globular mass of grass built 2 to 5 metres up in a bush or small tree.

Red Munia ***Amandava amandava***

Local name: Yerra jinuvayi (Telugu), Lal munia (Hindi) Size : 10 cm.

The male in the breeding season is bright red with white spots. The red in the female and non-breeding male is restricted to the beak, rump and upper tail coverts while the body is brownish with whitish marks . Both male and female have red bills. Usually found in flocks of about 30 or so. Frequents tall grasslands, marshes with reeds, sugarcane fields, etc. Roosts communally in reed beds and sugarcane fields. The nesting season is chiefly between June and October. The nest is a ball of grass, built within a metre from the ground, in a thorny bush or reed clump.

White-throated Munia [Indian Silverbill] ***Lonchura malabarica***

Local name: Jinuvayi (Telugu), Pidda (Hindi) Size : 11 - 11.5 cm.

This is a light brown coloured bird with a blue-grey bill, white rump and white under parts. Usually found in flocks of about 6 or larger in cultivated areas, dry grassland, open scrub, etc. Feeds on seeds – either picked off the ground or from seed heads. The nesting season is through the year. The nest is a large globular mass of grasses built 2 to 5 metres up in thick bushes. The nests are also used for roosting after the breeding season.

Baya Weaver
Ploceus philippinus
Local name: Pasapu pitta (Telugu), Baya, Son-chiri (Hindi)
Size : 15 cm.

This bird is rather hard to spot in the non-breeding season as it resembles the female house sparrow. In the breeding season, which is between May and September, the male dons a bright yellow plumage. Bayas are found in flocks near cultivated land – especially paddy and other cereal crop fields. But the bird is not an exclusive grain feeder, it also eats insects. The nest is what made the Baya famous as the weaver bird. The male weaves a suspended globular inverted retort-shaped nest from strips of leaves from paddy and other grasses. The nests take on a yellowish pale-brown colour as the grass dries. Half-made nests are inspected by prospective female partners. Only after the nest is approved, is it completed and given its final retort shape with its long entrance tube. The inside of the nest is often plastered with tiny lumps of mud – probably to add stability-giving weight to protect it from strong winds.

Streaked Weaver *Ploceus manyar*
Local name: Charal pichuka (Telugu), Bamani baya (Hindi) Size : 14 cm.

The crown in breeding males is yellow. The female and non-breeding males are brown. The under parts are boldly streaked with black. Found in grasslands and in reed beds. The call is a *chit-chit-chit*. It feeds on grass seeds. In the breeding season the males give vent to a jingling song, *tilili, tililee-kiti-tilileekiti*. The nesting season is between February and September. The retort-shaped woven nest is made of strips of paddy leaves and other grasses and is placed in a small colony in reed beds.

Yellow-throated Sparrow
Petronia xanthocollis
Local name: Adavi pichuka (Telugu), jangli chiriya (Hindi) Size : 13.5 cm.

This pale brownish grey sparrow has a lemon yellow 'thumb impression' on its breast in males and also some females. It also has two conspicuous chestnut coloured shoulder patches and white wing bars. Seen in open forest, scrub, edges of cultivation, etc. In the non-breeding season it can be found in large groups picking seeds off the ground. In the breeding season, it is usually seen in small parties in trees, feeding on plant material such as shoots and nectar, and on insects. Roosts in large groups. Calls often in the early mornings from the tops of tall trees. The nesting season is in the summer. The nest is a small pad of grass, wool, feathers, etc., stuffed inside a tree-hole.

House Sparrow *Passer domesticus*
Local name: Ooripichuka (Telugu), Gauriya (Hindi) Size : 15 cm.

A once familiar bird, its dwindling numbers in cities and towns are a cause of concern. The house sparrow has a grey crown, black throat and chest, streaked, chestnut brown mantle and white underparts. The female is buff , without the black markings on the face. Usually seen in flocks – many individuals gather at favourite trees and shrubs to roost. Call is a sweet sounding *chirrup, chirrup*. Food consists largely of seed, especially of cereals. Insects and young shoots are also eaten. Nesting season is practically throughout the year. Nest is a bulky dome of straw, stems, etc., placed in a hole or under the roof. Young ones are fed on insects and caterpillars.

Common Hill Myna
Gracula religiosa
Local name: Konga gorinka (Telugu), Pahari myna (Hindi) Size : 25 - 29 cm.

It is a large myna with yellow wattles and bill and white wing patches. Found in pairs or flocks in wooded hillsides. Keeps to trees, feeding on figs, berries, flower buds and insects. A great mimic and so a favourite of bird-fanciers. Also known as the "talking myna" for its ability to learn and repeat words. The nesting season is between March and October. The nest is a collection of grass, leaves, feathers, etc., in a tree hollow.

Common Myna
Acridotheres tristis
Local myna: Gorinka (Telugu), Myna (Hindi)
Size : 25 cm.

A brown bird with yellow orbitals, and white tail tip and wing patch, conspicuous in flight. Commensal of man, usually found in pairs or small groups. Feeds on fruit, insects, flower nectar, food refuse, etc. Looks out for earthworms exposed while ploughing, and insects disturbed by moving cattle. Roosts communally in large trees – sometimes in those standing right next to busy city roads – creating a huge din in the evening. The nesting season is between April and August. The nest is a collection of twigs, roots, paper and other rubbish in a hole in a tree or wall or in the space between mangled telephone wires on a pole.

Asian Pied Starling *Sturnus contra*

Local Name: Vendi pariki pitta, Venda gorinka (Telugu), Ablak (Hindi). Size : 23 cm.

A slim, black and white bird with yellow- orange bill and orbital skin. This bird is found in small flocks around cultivation, damp grasslands, garbage dumps, etc., often near human habitation. It feeds on cereal grains, fruit, flower nectar, and on insects that it digs out of damp ground. Roosts in large flocks. The breeding season is between March and October. A bulky nest made of twigs, leaves, grass and rubbish is built on the outer branches of a tree. In recent years, it has been extending its range westward in Andhra Pradesh and is now seen in and around Hyderabad.

Brahminy Starling *Sturnus pagodarum*

Local Name: Papata gorinki, Nalla topi pariki pitta (Telugu), Brahmani myna (Hindi). Size : 21 cm.

This is a reddish fawn bird with a grey back. It has a glossy black crown. Its name is derived from its colour which is reminiscent of a hermit's(or brahmin's) robes. Small flocks are seen in moist grasslands, cultivation, scrub and dry deciduous forests. They eat berries, figs and insects.The breeding season is from May to July. It nests in tree hollows or ruined walls.

Rosy Starling

Sturnus roseus

Local Name: Gulabi parikipitta (Telugu), Gulabi myna (Hindi). Size: 23cm.

A dull-pink bird with a black head, wings and tail. Winter migrant. Plumage brighter in breeding season. Found in huge flocks, often near cultivation. It feeds on insect pests, crops like jowar, fruits of banyan, peepul, lantana, etc.

Racket-tailed Drongo *Dicrurus paradiseus*
Local name: Goppa chattathoka etrintha , Tinka passala poligadu (Telugu), Bhimraj, Bhangraj (Hindi) Size : 32 cm.

This glossy black bird has a prominent tufted forehead and two rackets at the tip of its tail, which look as though two dark bees are pursuing the bird in flight. Found in forests, this is a very noisy bird with loud metallic calls. It is also a good mimic of other birds' calls. It feeds on moths, other insects and flower nectar. The nesting season is between February and July. The nest is a deep cup of fine twigs, rootlets and fibres woven together and bound to an end fork in a branch with cobwebs.

Black Drongo *Dicrurus macrocercus*
Local Name: Nalla etrintha (Telugu), Kolsa, Kotwal, Zulfikar (Hindi) Size: 30 cm.

The is a slim, compact built, glossy black bird with a deeply forked tail. It perches on telephone lines, fences, etc., hunting winged insects. Insects are seized, carried back to the perch, torn up and eaten. Open bush and scrub set on fire invariably attract drongos which prey on the fleeing insects. They also drink nectar from flowers of trees such as the silk cotton. The call is a harsh "*ti-tiu*" and "*cheece-cheece-chichuk*". The drongo is a bold bird – other smaller birds build their nests close to that of a drongo for the protection it offers from predators. It nests between April and August. The nest is a cup of fine twigs and fibres cemented with cobweb, snugly placed in the extreme fork of the branch of a large isolated tree.

Eurasian Golden Oriole

Oriolus oriolus

Local name: Vangu pandu (Telugu), Peelak (Hindi). Size : 25 cm.

This bright yellow bird with the black *kajal* mark is locally migratory. It can be spotted in places where there are trees and is generally found in pairs. The female is dull and greener. It has two calls – one harsh, and the other, a melodious "*pee-lo-lo*". The Golden Oriole feeds on figs, berries, insects, caterpillars, and nectar of blossoms of flowering trees such as the coral tree. The nesting season is between April and August. The nest is a neatly woven cup of grass and fibres snugly fitted into the fork of a branch.

Indian Tree-Pie *Dendrocitta vagabunda*

Local Name: Yerra gokuraayi (Telugu), Mahalat (Hindi). Size : 46 - 50 cm.

This smart cousin of the crow frequents large gardens with trees and is also found in wooded country and scrubland. It is a long tailed, chestnut-brown bird with a sooty grey head and grey tail tipped with black. Juveniles have brown heads.Usually found in pairs or in a small group in a tree. Utters both harsh calls as well as pleasant ones (a loud, flute-like *ko-ki-la*). Feeds on fruit, insects, lizards, frogs, centipedes, young birds, mice, etc. The nesting season is between February and July. The nest is made of twigs and is lined with rootlets.

Jungle Crow *Corvus macrorhynchos*
Local Name: Nalla Kaaki (Telugu), Jungli Kowwa (Hindi)
Size : 46 - 59 cm.

This is a glossy jet black bird with a heavy bill and a domed head. It is more common in villages and in the open countryside, forests and cultivation than in urban areas. It frequently scavenges on dead animals – in jungles on the kills of large predators – and is commonly seen in the company of vultures. It is however omnivorous and is not dependant on carrion. The nesting season is between December and April. The nests are often parasaitised by the Koel.

House Crow *Corvus splendens*
Local Name: Kaaki, Manchi kaaki (Telugu), Kowwa (Hindi)
Size : 40 cm.

One of our most familiar birds. The grey neck and smaller size distinguish it from the all- black Jungle Crow. It is an omnivore and is hence a useful scavenger. Crows have communal roots – several dozens gather at the same tree or group of trees every evening. The nesting season is between April and June. The nest is a platform of twigs reinforced with several handy materials picked up from its human neighbours – iron wire, plastic pieces, coir fibres, etc. Koels commonly lay their eggs in crows' nests.

MAMMALS

In our daily parlance, we associate the word 'animal' with all four legged creatures, while 'mammals' are warm blooded, furry animals that give birth to live young ones and feed milk to them.

There are about 5,000 species of living mammals. They are divided into three subclasses and about 26 orders (though there is no consensus among biologists on the exact number of orders). Unlike other animals, mammals have body hair, have 3 middle ear bones (the malleus, incus, and stapes), and nourish their young with milk that females produce in modified sweat glands that are called mammary glands. The scientific classification for mammals mentioned in this book follows Wilson and Reeder (1993).

All mammals fall in the class Mammalia of the Phylum Vertebrata of the Kingdom Animalia. The following table describes the mammal orders and families that are represented in Andhra Pradesh and find mention in this book:

Orders of Class Mammalia	Families	Description
Primates	Loridae Cercopithecidae	Slender Loris Macaques and Langurs
Artiodactyla (Even-toed hoofed mammals)	Cervidae Bovidae Suidae	Deer and Chevortains Gaur, antelopes Wild boars
Proboscidea	Elephantidae	Elephants
Carnivora	Ursidae Canidae Hyaenidae Felidae Mustelidae Viverridae Herpestidae	Bears Dog family including wolves, jackals, foxes Hyena Cat family including tigers, leopards and wild cats Badgers, otters and weasels Civets Mongoose
Pholidota	Manidae	Scaly ant eaters or Pangolins
Lagomorpha	Leporidae	Hares, rabbits
Insectivora	Erinacidae Soricidae	Hedgehogs Shrews
Rodentia	Sciuridae Muridae Hystericidae	Squirrels Rats and mice Porcupines
Chiroptera	Pteropodiacea Megadermatidae	Fruit bats False vampire bats

PARTS OF A MAMMAL

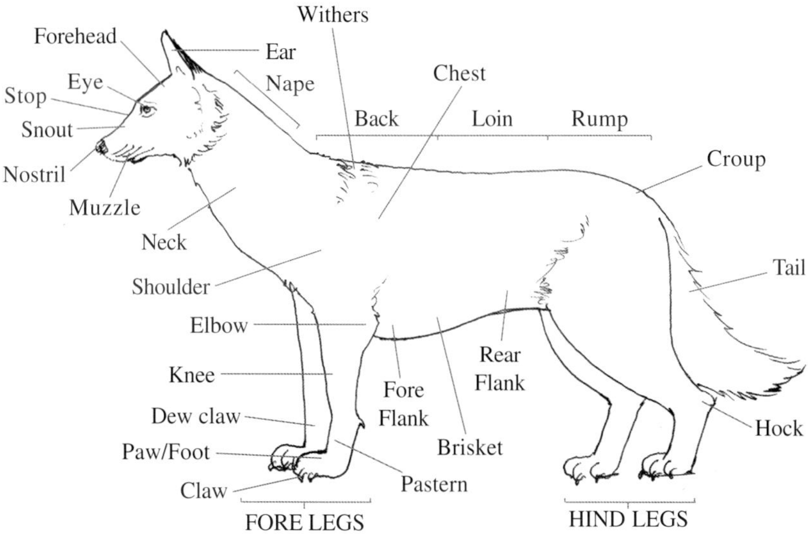

Slender Loris

Loris targiradus

Local Name: Devanga Pilli (Telugu).

Size: Length of the head and body is 20-25 cm. The male weighs 280-340 g while the female weighs 225 g.

This secretive creature appears as a small ball of soft fur when tightly curled up in a tree hole or branches as it sleeps during the day. It is very thin and lanky with long slender limbs, has huge owl like eyes set in a dark patch, white muzzle with a pointed snout and prominent ears. Its fur is soft and greyish (or reddish brown in the young). It has no tail. Its forelimbs have movable thumbs, which possess a highly specialized pincer like grip.

It moves slowly adopting a stealthy approach to grab the prey with both hands. It feeds on berries of *Lantana* bushes, insects, geckos, small birds and tree frogs. It marks its territory by soaking its hands and feet with its own urine, thereby leaving a scent trail wherever it moves. It leads a solitary life, freely inhabiting the open tree jungles instead of confining itself to the dense forests. Its eyes cannot tolerate bright sunlight. The habitat preferred by these animals, is constantly being taken over by humans thereby threatening its survival. These animals are constantly captured and sold for their eyes, which are said to be potent love charms and are believed to cure eye diseases. Survival of these animals can be ensured if their preferred habitat is maintained, and by clearing the myths and superstitions related to them. They are sometimes seen in pairs. The gestation period is over 3 months. Usually, 1-2 young ones are produced, which are nursed for long periods.

Bonnet Macaque
Macaca radiata
Local Names: Kothi (Telugu), Bandar (Hindi).

Size: Seated, the Bonnet Macaque is less than 2 ft high. Males weigh 6-9 kg, while females weigh 3-4 kg.

A long tailed monkey with no whiskers (except straggling hair) or beard, and a cap of long dark hair, radiating from a whorl on the crown, which is short and neatly parted in the center of the forehead. It is brown in colour but paler below, with a flesh coloured face and a very low cast look, with a tail as long as the head and body. The coat is lustrous olive brown to buff grey.

It lives in highly organized troops with well-defined territories. It is a good swimmer. It feeds on fruits, berries, leaves and shoots, and also insects, grubs and spiders. It has cheek pouches into which it crams large quantities of extra food, which can be consumed later. Males play a dominant role in the social structure. Mating occurs throughout the year, with a peak in October-November. A major birth season precedes the monsoon from January to late April. The average life span is 12-15 years.

Rhesus Macaque

Macaca mulatta

Local Names: Kothi (Telugu), Bandar (Hindi).

Size: The average adult male is about 2 ft high and weighs 10 kg. Females are smaller and lighter. Tail is not more than half the length of the head and body.

The most distinctive character is the brown coat, which becomes reddish or yellowish at the back. Hindquarters are naked round the seat pads. Face and other bare parts are flesh coloured or red (as seen mostly in older females). It possesses short close side-whiskers, but no beard. Hair on the head is seen lying straight back.

Although some of them live habitually among rocks and cliffs and in jungles, where they prefer open country, they are also found in towns and villages, near temples, wells and groves. It is a good swimmer. It feeds mainly on the ground. It is an omnivorous creature and its food mainly consists of plants, insects, grub and spiders. Male dominance is prominent in the social structure. Mating occurs throughout the year (October-December being the most favorable period). The pre-monsoon (March-June) and post-monsoon period (September-October) are the major birth seasons.

Common Langur or Hanuman Monkey
Semnopithecus entellus

Local Names: Kondamucchu (Telugu), Langur, Hanuman (Hindi).

Size: Seated, it measures 2 to 2.5 ft high. Tail is 3 to 3.25 ft long. It weights 9-16 kg.

It is a long limbed, long tailed, black-faced monkey. The body is pale dirty and straw coloured, or ashy grey, darker on the shoulders and rump, paler on the head and lower parts. Hands, feet and face are black.

It is mainly arboreal in habitat, living in deciduous forests (particularly dry tropical forests, scrub jungles, arid rocky areas with xerophytic vegetation), towns, villages and temples. The langur is herbivorous, feeding on wild fruits, flowers, buds, shoots and leaves. It starts feeding at dawn. Its chief predators are leopards, tigers and crocodiles. It sleeps in a squatting position on the extremities of branches. Langurs live in troops of 15, with well-established territories. Adult males act as troop leaders. A female may give birth every 2 years. The gestation period is 6 months. The peak birth period is January-February.

Sambar

Cervus unicolor

Local Names: Karimegam, Peda duppi, Kanuzu, Kadathi (Telugu), Sambar, Samar (Hindi).

Size: Sambar is the largest of all Indian deer. A full-grown male sambar measures 140 cm at the shoulder and weighs 225-320 kg.

This deer is characterized by impressive antlers and a massively built body with a coarse coat, which is brown in colour with a yellowish or greyish tinge above and paler underparts. Females are lighter in colour. In stags, there is a heavy mane around the neck and throat. The antlers are stout and rugged. The brow tine is set at an acute angle with the beam. Near the tip, the beam bifurcates into two nearly equally long tines. The average length of the antlers is 65-75 cm.

It inhabits the forested hill tracts and wooded areas. It feeds on grass, leaves and various kinds of wild fruits and comes out to feed only after dusk. It has a highly well developed sense of smell and hearing. It is a good swimmer. The antlers are cast between March – April and regrowth commences in May. Males fight for territory. Each herd consists of 4-12 animals. Mating takes place in November-December. Soon after the rut, the stag deserts the harem and leads a solitary life. The young ones are born just before monsoons.

Front Foot

Chital or Spotted Deer

Axis axis

Local names: Duppi, Jinka (Telugu), Chital (Hindi).

Size: An average chital grows to 90 cm at the shoulder and weighs about 85 kg.

The Chital, which is endemic to India, is perhaps the most beautiful of all deer. Its coat is a bright rufous-fawn, having white spots at all ages and in all seasons. Older individuals are darker in shade.They are ruminants with solid antlers. The graceful antlers have 3 tines.

Chital is found wherever there is jungle that is combined with good grazing and plentiful supply of water. They are seen in herds of 10-30, which may contain 2-3 stags. They feed till late in the morning and again in the afternoon and lie down during intervals in some shady spot. Chitals are prolific breeders. The rutting stag has a loud harsh bellow and combats between stags for the possession of hinds are fierce and frequent. Usually the hind (female) gives birth to a single fawn. The stags shed and regrow their antlers periodically. The newly grown antlers are encased in a thick soft skin called 'velvet', which is highly sensitive and easily injured. The chital takes great care to avoid any harm to them. When the antlers have reached their maximum length, a ring of bony matter called 'burr' forms just above the point where the antler unites with its base and cuts off blood supply. As a result, the velvet shrinks, dries and eventually gets peeled off due to frequent rubbing by the deer. Feeding conditions influence antler shedding. Chitals mainly eat grasses, which contain abundant calcium, useful for formation of bones. In the hornless hinds, this excess calcium is utilized to provide for the developing embryo and the protracted nursing of the young ones. The principal predators of chital are tigers, leopards and wild dogs. Chitals lead a very social life amidst langurs, wild cattle, pigs, mynas, and many species. Since they inhabit the open country on the fringes of the forests, where the visibility is less limited, all their faculties are uniformly developed. Alertness, a premonition of danger, quickened by a keen sense of scent, hearing and sight, and the speed of movement are chital's essential means of escape.When alarmed, the chital raises its tail, to display its white undertail. This signals other chital to flee.

The Barking Deer or Muntjac

Muntiacus muntjac

Local names: Kuka gorre, Morugu jinka (Telugu), Kakar (Hindi).

Size: The average adult weighs 20-23 kg and measures 50-75 cm at the shoulder. The horns do not exceed 13 cm in length and are shed between May-June.

Distinctive Characters: This small deer is characterized by a close, sleek reddish or chestnut brown coat with small antlers, consisting of a short brow tine and an unbranched beam, which are set on bony hair covered pedicles extending down each side of the face like a bony ridge. Instead of antlers, females have tufts of spiny hair.

Habits: It occupies the wooded hills and avoids thick jungles. It feeds on leaves, grasses and wild fruits. When heard from a distance, its call resembles a dog bark. It breeds throughout the year. Just at the beginning of the rains, 2 young ones are born.

Front Foot, 3cm

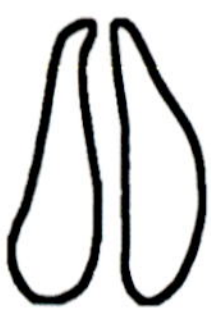

Chevrotain or Mouse Deer

Tragulus mimenna

Front Foot

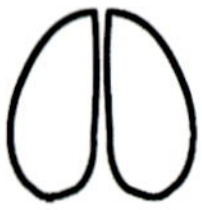

Local names: Mooshika Jinka (Telugu), Pisora, Pisura (Hindi).

Size: It measures 25-30 cm in height at the shoulders.

This tiny little shy deer is characterized by slender limbs, high hindquarters, prominent tusks, olive brown coat with minute yellow spots and 3 white stripes on the throat .The flank is marked with rows of white or buff coloured spots, which extend into longitudinal bands over its body. The underparts are whitish. The eyes are large and surrounded by a white patch. It has a 3-chambered stomach (replacing the 4 chambered stomach found in other ruminants) and 4 well developed toes on each foot with bones of side toes being complete. This is in contrast to other ruminants, in which some of these bones are imperfect and missing.

It lives in grass covered rocky hillsides or in forests, concealing itself under large boulders or under rock crevices. It comes out of its shelter to feed in the mornings and at dusk. The males lead a solitary life except during the pairing season. Two young ones are born at the end of the monsoon.

Chinkara or Indian Gazelle

Gazella bennettii

Local names: Burra Jinka, Gaddi Jinka (Telugu), Chinkara, Kal Punch (Hindi).

Size: An average adult stands 65 cm tall at the shoulders and weighs about 23 kg. Females are smaller.

This graceful gazelle is characterized by a light chestnut coloured body, with the colour deepening near the white underparts on the buttocks and the flanks. A white streak runs down each side of the face with a dusky patch above the nose. The horns in males are S-shaped and possess 15-25 rings while the horns of females are smooth. The average length of the horns is 25-30 cm in males and 10-13 cm in females. Few females are hornless.

Chinkara live in arid and semi-arid areas, thin jungles and sand dunes of the desert zones. Being shy of human beings, they come out late in the evenings. They mainly feed on grasses, leaves, crops and fruits. They can go without water for long periods. The usual herd size is between 3-25. The male demarcates its territory of about 200 m diameter using fecal heaps. Although there is no breeding season in particular, two birth peaks are observed – a major one in April, and a minor one in autumn. The gestation period is 5 months.

Black Buck

Antilope cervicapra

Local names: Krishna Jinka (Telugu), Harna (*Male)*, Harni (*Female*), Mrig (Hindi).

Size: An average buck weighs about 25-45 kg.

Males have a dark brown to black coat colour and 20-25 inches long straight horns, which are loosely wound about the longitudinal axis, with ridges across.Sexual dimorphism is distinct. Females are usually hornless.

They occur in practically all the plain areas and avoid forest or hill tracts. Black bucks remain in groups of 15-50 individuals. As the young males approach maturity, they are driven from the herd and form bachelor parties among themselves. Usually the herd is led by an old vigilant female. Their sense of hearing is moderate whereas that of scent is fairly well developed. They have a keen eyesight and run at a very high speed. When a herd of black bucks is alarmed, a single member bounds into the air to a surprising height, and is soon followed by another, until the whole herd is in motion. These bounds are continued for a few strides after which the herd settles to a regular gallop. Black bucks feed almost throughout the day, resting in the shade during the hottest part of the afternoon. The short grass along with various cereal crops is the chief food of these bucks. They breed in all seasons but main rut takes place in February-March. They are particularly pugnacious at this time. A buck then struts about with a peculiar, mincing gait, uttering short, challenging grunts, with its head thrown upwards and horns parallel to its back.

Four-Horned Antelope or Chowsingha
Tetracerus quadricornis

Local names: Konda Gorre (Telugu), Chowsingha, Chowka, Jungli Bakri (Hindi).

Size: It is the smallest antelope in Asia.The height of the average male is 65 cm at the shoulder level and weighs 16 kg.

The most striking feature of Chowsingha is the presence of two pairs of horns. The coat is dull reddish brown above and white below with a dark stripe running down the front of each leg (which is more prominent in the foreleg). Old bucks are often yellowish. The posterior horns are usually 8-10 cm long and the anterior ones are just 1-1.25 cm long. It has a pair of well-developed glands between the false hooves of the hind legs in both the sexes.

It occupies the wooded and hilly tracts and avoids the dense forests. It prefers the tall grass and open jungles. It gives a low whistling call, which is repeated in hot weather. But when alarmed, it gives out a different call, which is similar to a dog bark, but much softer. It is extremely dependent on water. It lives alone or sometimes in pairs. The breeding season is in summer and during monsoon. Two young ones are born after a gestation period of about 8 months.

Nilgai or Blue Bull

Boselaphus tragocamelus

Local names: Manu bothu (Telugu), Nilgai, Roz, Rojra, Nil (Hindi).

It is a large animal with a horse-like build, high withers and low rump. The bull has a coarse iron grey coat while the female and the calves have chestnut or tawny coats. It has a white ring below each fetlock and two white spots on each cheek. The chin, lips, inside of the ears and the undersurfaces of the tail are white. Dark short manes are present in both sexes. The male has a distinct tuft of stiff black hairs on the throat and stout cone like keeled horns with a triangular base and circular tips. The average height of males is 130 – 140 cm, while females are much smaller. The horns measure 20 cm.

It inhabits the barren hills or plain scrublands and avoids dense forests. It feeds till late in the morning and after a brief period of rest from the afternoon heat, again commences feeding early in the evening. It is a grazer as well as a browser, feeding on leaves, fruits, flowers, etc. It can do without water for long periods. It has a good sense of smell and sight. It lives in herds comprising of 4-10 cows, calves, and younger bulls. The young ones are produced at all seasons after a gestation period of 8-9 months.

Front Foot

Gaur or Indian Bison

Bos gaurus

Local names: Adavi dunna, Gorregeda (Telugu), Gaur, Gaur gai (Hindi)

Being the tallest living oxen and one of the heaviest land mammals in India, the Gaur, with a huge head, massive body, and sturdy limbs, is one of the most magnificent ungulates. An adult gaur bull weighs 700-900 kg and stands 1.6-1.9 m at shoulder height. It has a prominent muscular ridge upon its shoulder, which slopes down to the middle of the back and ends in an abrupt dip. The sharp pointed crescent shaped horns are cream in colour and usually tipped with black. The feet are white or slightly yellow coloured upto the knee. Old bulls have black and almost hairless bodies with an ashy forehead. It is a hill animal with an acute sense of smell and good hearing but with poor sight. It grazes on the green grass during the monsoon and during the dry season it feeds on leaves of trees, shrubs, bamboo shoots, buds and herbs. It often visits 'salt licks' where the soil is impregnated with salts and minerals. It is non-territorial, sharing its habitat with other members of the same species. It lives in small herds of 8-12 animals. The hierarchy, which is based on the size and age, ensures that high-ranking males have the first call on females in season. The mating period is from November-March. After a gestation period of 8-9 months, the cow gives birth to a single calf. The average life span is supposed to be 30 years. As per Schedule I of the Indian Wildlife (Protection) Act, 1972, Gaur is an endangered and protected animal. Its only predator is the tiger, but the herds are periodically decimated by parasites, causing various diseases.

Front Foot, 15cm

Indian Pangolin (Scaly Anteater)
Manis crassicaudata

Local names: Alawa (Telugu),Bajra kit, Bajra kapta, Suraj mukhi, Silu, Sal sala (Hindi).

The most distinctive character of the Indian Pangolin is the armor of protecting scales over its body. These overlapping large scales may be regarded as modified hairs or spines, which are enormously enlarged and flattened. The body is light fawn or olive coloured with fleshy underparts. It measures about 2 ft in length of head and body while the tail is 15 to 20 inches long. Being nocturnal, it spends daytime in burrows dug by it. Curved and blunted claws on its feet (which are far more prominent and longer in its forefeet) facilitate excavation.

Pangolins feed on ants and termites. Being toothless, it licks and swallows the ants and termites using its glutinous tongue. It is particularly fond of the large leaf nests of the big red tree ants. Although it is known to drink water freely by the rapid in and out movement of its tongue, it can go without water for a very long time. When excited, it makes a loud hissing sound. Its sense of hearing and sight are poor but the sense of smell is very well developed. The animal walks with its back well arched and tail held off the ground. In defense, the pangolin curls itself up into an armored ball, which is difficult to unroll. A single young one or rarely two are produced each time. Both the parents take care of it. Hill tribes eat the flesh of pangolins and the scales are made into rings as a charm against rheumatic diseases.

Indian Wildboar or Wild Pig
Sus cristatus

Local names: Adavi pandi (Telugu), Jangli Suar, Barba, Badajanwar, Burajanwar (Hindi).

A typical well-grown wild boar weighs 230 kg and measures 3 ft in height with a coarse coat, which develops into a crest on the spine and becomes thinner down the back. The wild boar is blackish grey or rusty brown with white hairs on its body. The young ones have black or dark brown stripes. The upper and lower tusks or 'tushes' curve outward and project from the mouth. This intelligent and ferocious animal generally lives in scrub jungles, grasslands and forest areas. Being omnivorous, their diet ranges from insects, snakes and carrions to crops, roots and tubers. They feed early in the morning and the evenings. It is very destructive to crops in cultivated areas. They have a very good sense of smell while sense of hearing and sight is moderate. They are prolific breeders, breeding throughout the year. At the end of the gestation period of 4 months, 4-6 young ones are born.

Front Foot, 5cm

Asian Elephant
Elephas maximus

Local names: Yenugu (Telugu), Hathi (*Male*), Hathini (*Female*) (Hindi).

The largest mammal to walk on the surface of Earth since prehistoric times, throughout Africa, Europe and the Asian mainland, the elephant is at the crossroads of survival today. Of the more than 300 species of tusked animals, the elephant remains the sole survivor. Elephants are highly social creatures. The female giving birth is attended by another female (aunt). There is only one baby but twins occur occasionally. They protect the baby if danger is apprehended by clustering around it, helping it to keep up with the herd, and disciplining it if its playfulness gets out of hand. An elephant's trunk is its most intriguing organ, primarily a nose for breathing. It is also a pneumatic hose capable of sucking and blowing liquid when drinking and showering, and to collect dust to blow over the body. It serves as a trumpet and a sounding board. As a highly flexible working tool, it is almost as versatile as our hands. Trumpeting is the most common elephant sound. But elephants also produce deep rumbles, barks, cries and snorts. An important recent discovery is that they communicate through infra sound. Such extraordinary creatures, which monopolized large parts of India, now exist in isolated pockets and are at the verge of extinction. They are threatened by poaching, habitat destruction and development schemes. Unless we ensure conservation priorities, we will snap our centuries old bond with this majestic creature that has been depicted in the Paleolithic rock paintings, and even on the seals of Indus Valley Civilization.

Front Foot

Sloth Bear

Melursus ursinus

Local names: Reench (Hindi), Elugu Bunti, Guddelugu (Telugu).

It is a long, shaggy, nocturnal animal with blackish brown fur, small eyes, a protruding snout and large loose lips. The tips of its feet and muzzle are dirty white or yellowish, while the claws (which are always longer on the forefeet) are ivory white. The breast is ornamented with a white coloured V-shaped patch. It usually attains a height of 2 m. It has broad, naked soled feet, which helps it secure a better grip on tree trunks and branches. It prefers living away from human habitation, in the forests, where there is sufficient food. It is nocturnal and hunts at night. Being omnivorous, it feeds mainly on fruits and insects. It is particularly fond of honey and termites, which are sucked out from the termite hills using the mobile and protrusible lips, which are modified for suction. Its sense of smell is highly developed, while those of sight and hearing are poor. It is a good swimmer. Being a thirsty creature, it requires a constant supply of water. Unlike in the cold countries where the bears are forced to hibernate due to shortage of food, sloth bears in our state do not hibernate, but remain active throughout the year. Mating occurs in summer. Around 1-3 small, blind and hairless young ones are born in winter after a gestation period of 7 months. The mother is very aggressive when accompanied by its cub. Except when mating, or accompanied by the cubs, it leads a solitary life. The care of the cubs is the responsibility of the mother as the male deserts its mate soon after mating.

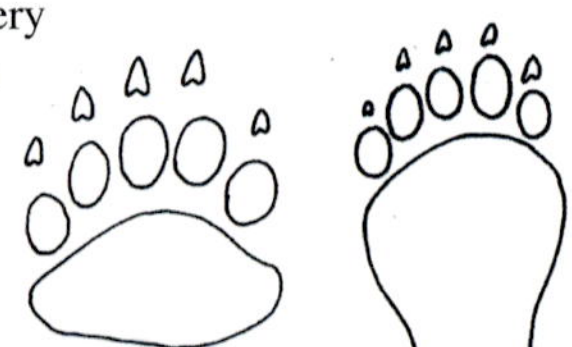

Forepaw ***Hindpaw, 15cm***

Wolf

Canis lupus

Local Names: Thodelu (Telugu), Bheriya, Nekra, Bighana, Hundar, Hurar (Hindi).

It is larger than a medium (pariah) dog, with large ears, an arching brow, an elevated forehead, a large skull, has yellow eyes and a bushy tail almost half the length of the head and body. The sandy fawn coat is clouded with black. Cubs are sooty brown with a white patch on the chest. An adult male stands 65-75 cm at the shoulder. The body length is 90-105 cm and it weighs 18-27 kg. It occupies bare, open areas as well as forests, living in caves and cavities of the rocks. It hunts during the day or at night. It preys on cattle, hunts black bucks, birds, and smaller animals like hares. Breeding takes place in winters. The litter consists of 3-9 whelps. The average life span is 12-15 years.

Jackal

Canis aureus

Local Names: Nakka (Telugu), Gidhad, Kola (Hindi).

It is smaller than an ordinary pariah dog, with shorter ears and a bushy tail with a tan coat mixed with black. The tip of the tail is black. Full-grown individuals measure 38-43 cm in height, the length of head and body is 60-75 cm, while tail measures 20-27 cm. It weighs 8-11 kg. It gives out a long, eerie howl after nightfall. It lives in humid forests, dry open plains, deserts and occupies holes in the ground in dense scrub and grass. It is a nocturnal creature. Although they are scavengers by habit, feeding on dead bodies, a pack of jackals can also hunt a deer or an antelope or individually hunt poultry birds, hares, rats, goats and sheep. It also eats fallen fruits. It lives alone or in pairs. Cubs are born throughout the year in any natural shelter. The average life span is 12 years.

Indian Fox

Vulpes bengalensis

Local names: Gunta Nakka, Konka Nakka (Telugu), Lomri (Hindi)

The Indian fox is as large as a cat, with large ears, slender nose and limbs, which are rufous while the rest of the fur is grey coloured. Its tail is 25-35 cm long, bushy and tipped with black. The underparts are lighter in tone. The head and body length is 45-60 cm, while the average weight is 1.8-3.2 kg. It prefers wastelands, scrublands and rocky hills rather than forests, occupying burrows dug by itself. The burrow is provided with several openings. This fox is nocturnal. It feeds on smaller mammals, reptiles, rats, land crabs, insects such as termites, and even certain fruits. Breeding occurs in the cold weather with usually 4 cubs being born in February-April, after a gestation period of 50-53 days. Both the parents care for the young ones.

Dhole or Indian Wild Dog

Cuon alpinus

Local names: Dhole, Rezu Kukka, Adavi Kukka (Telugu), Jangli Kutta, Ban Kutta (Hindi).

The Indian wild dog resembles a domestic dog in size, having a bright rust red coat with lighter underparts, rounded ears, bushy tail with a purple-black tip and hair between the toes. It is easily distinguished from the other members of the dog family in having 6 molars instead of 7 and 12-14 teats instead of the usual 10. An adult measures 43-55 cm at the shoulder. Length of the head and body measures 90 cm while the tail is 40-43 cm long. Males weigh about 20 kg while females are lighter. It lives in forests in packs of 10-15 individuals. It has a strong sense of smell and sight. It usually preys on wild pigs and deer. Large packs may even hunt gaur and bears. The pack tires out the prey, tears and eats it up. It breeds in winter. Several females may breed in a colony. Usually 4-6 cubs are born in January-February.

Common Mongoose

Herpestes edwardsi

Local names: Mungisa (Telugu), Mangus, Newal, Newara (Hindi).

It is yellowish grey in colour with the grizzled coat having a 'pepper and salt' tinge. Its yellow-red tipped tail is as long as the body the tip. It is about 90 cm long of which the tail measures 45 cm. It weighs about 1.4 kg. It occupies the open scrublands, hedgerows and thickets. It lives under the rocks or bushes or in the hollows of a tree trunk. It has a diurnal habit. It feeds on rice, mice, snakes, lizards, frogs, bird eggs, insects and even on plant roots and fruits. It also feeds on carrion. About 3 young ones are born in a litter after a gestation period of 60 days.

Striped Hyena

Hyaena hyaena

Local names: Dumul gundu, Korna gundu, Kondrigadu (Telugu), Hundar, Lakkar baghar, Teras (Hindi).

The striped hyena is a large animal, dog like in general form, with blunt non-retractile claws, dark eyes, long moustaches and a striped coat with mane running all down the neck and back. The colour of the coat varies from cream, buff, tawny to grey. Tail is striped with black or brown. It has a broad head with large, pointed ,upstanding ears. The forelimbs are sturdy and long but the hindquarters are weak and drooping. It has an extremely powerful set of jaws. On an average it measures about 150 cm in length and 90 cm in height. Males weigh 35-40 kg while females weigh about 30-35 kg. It is generally found in open country, rocky scrub covered hills, deserts and is found living in holes or caves during daytime. It is a nocturnal animal that feeds on carrion and prey killed by other animals. Its shelter is usually littered with its peculiar dung composed of crushed bone, dried into hard white balls. It gives out a loud, harsh, unearthly laughing chatter. It feigns death as an instinctive reaction under stress of attack. Mating takes place in winter. 3-4 young ones are born during the summer. Its average life span is about 16 years.

8cm

Tiger

Panthera tigris

Local Names: Pedda Pulee (Telugu), Bagh (Hindi)

Size: The average length is 280 cm (male) and 260 cm (female). The average weight is 180 – 230 kg (male) and 185 kg (female).

The tiger has a bright orange coat with black stripes, black ears, each with one white spot and a long, banded tail.The tiger prefers deciduous, thorn and evergreen forests, mangroves and grasslands, where it blends seamlessly with its surroundings due to its excellent camouflage.Usually tigers are identified by their telltale signs such as pugmarks and scrape marks. A tiger's pugmarks show the impression of only the toes and the great pad behind them. There is no trace of sole or heel because it walks on its toes. A tiger's jaws, its claws, and the great canine teeth are perfectly adapted to seize, hold and kill prey. When hunting, the eyes and ears guide a tiger.Its stripes provide a good camouflage. An adult tiger requires 3500 kg of prey per year, which it takes in around 43 kills (an equivalent of 1 buffalo, 2 cows, 3 sambar, 4 barasingha, 5 gaur, and 28 chitals). To escape heat, tigers take shelter in caves or lie partly submerged in water. A tigeress gives birth to her young in caves or under a rough shelter of rocks. The cubs are usually born blind and helpless. The tigress looks after the cubs while the tiger deserts the family before or soon after the cubs are born. Unfortunately, the tiger is hunted for its presumed superstitious medicinal and magical properties. Another threat is the shrinking of its habitat.

14cm

9cm

Common Leopard
Panthera pardus

Local names: Chiruta Puli (Telugu), Tendua (Hindi).

It is a sleek, short-haired animal with a fulvous or bright coat marked with small close-set black rosettes. A leopard lives in an open forest, as well as in thick forests. It is very watchful and stealthy with well-developed sight and hearing powers. Leopards around villages feed on cattle, sheep, poultry, goats and dogs, whereas in the forest leopards prey on deer, monkeys, porcupines, birds and reptiles. Its ability to climb trees with ease enables it to attack arboreal animals. The average adult male is 7 feet long, and weighs 65-70 kg, while the female is a foot shorter and weighs 50-55 kg. It follows the tracks of animals through the forest or awaits its prey in hiding. It leaps on its prey and seizes it by the throat until the prey dies of suffocation. It then drags its prey up a tree or to some other place of security, where it can feed upon it leisurely. A leopard breeds throughout the year. The gestation period is about 90 days. 2-4 blind cubs are born at a time. A leopard with a very dark coloured coat is referred to as a black panther.The leopard, being endangered, is presently being protected in over 200 sanctuaries and national parks in India.

Leopard Cat

Prionailurus bengalensis

Local names: Chiruta gurtulugala pilli (Telugu), Chitah Billi (Hindi).

The leopard cat is almost the size of a domestic cat and is characterized by a yellowish brown body, with black or dark brown spots and whitish underparts. The spots are arranged to form a regular line along the body or may merge into longitudinal bands. It has four distinct bands running from the crown over the neck, which forms elongated spots on the shoulder. A pair of horizontal cheek stripes is quite prominent. Its head and body measures 60 cm and it weighs 3-4 kg. It lives in forests, occupying tree hollows. It preys upon small birds and animals. It is nocturnal in habit. About 3-4 cubs are born in a litter between March and May.

Fishing Cat or Large Tiger Cat

Prionailurus viverrina

Local names: Chapalu Tiney Pilli (Telugu), Bagh-dasha, Banbiral, Khupyah – Bagh, Baraun (Hindi).

The fishing cat is one of our lesser cats, much bigger than a domestic cat, with a longer head and a shorter tail. Its fur is short, coarse and dull earthy grey with elongated brownish black spots of varying sizes and distinctness. The lower parts of the body are spotted. Its tail has distinct black rings. Head and body measure about 70 -100 cm while the tail is about 30 cm in length. The adult weighs between 11 and 15 kg. It usually lives close to water bodies from where it derives its food, usually fish and waterfowl. It also kills birds, dogs, sheep and calves. It is very common in the mangrove forests of Andhra Pradesh. Its method of fishing is to crouch on a rock or overhanging bank and to scoop up fish with its paws. It gives birth to 2 – 3 cubs in a litter. It is listed as an endangered species.

Jungle Cat

Felis chaus

Local names: Junca Pilli (Telugu), Khatas, Jungli billi (Hindi).

The jungle cat is larger than a domestic cat, with longer legs and a short tail that ends above the hock. Ears often have a rudimentary tuft. The general colour is light reddish grey or greyish brown, with few or no dark markings except 2 to 3 dark stripes on the upper forelimbs, a black tail tip and a few rings preceding it. The eye has a black tear stripe. Head and body measure 2 ft in length while the tail is less than 1 ft long. It weighs around 6 kg. Completely black specimens are occasionally found. It frequents open country and grass cover, crops, woodlands, while hunting for birds and small mammals. The females bear litters of three kittens each in January-April and August-November.

Common Otter

Lutra lutra

Local names: Neeti Kukka (Telugu), Ud, Ud bilao, Pani Kutta (Hindi).

The common otter is a large otter with a rough coat, dark brown with whitish cheeks, throat and underparts. It has a close coat with waterproof fur, a thick muscular tail, paddle like feet and a naked snout with bristle-like whiskers. The body is streamlined and almost cylindrical. The head is broad and flattened. Head and body measures 60-80 cm in length, while the tail is about 45 cm long. It lives in cool streams, lakes and estuaries, occupying the hollow areas beneath the rocks, boulders and roots of trees near edges of water. It feeds on fish, crabs, crustaceans, frogs, rodents and waterfowl. It usually hunts at night. It lives in a group or a family. Mating occurs in water. The gestation period is 61 days. Its nursery, called a 'Holt' is usually a burrow dug at the water edge.

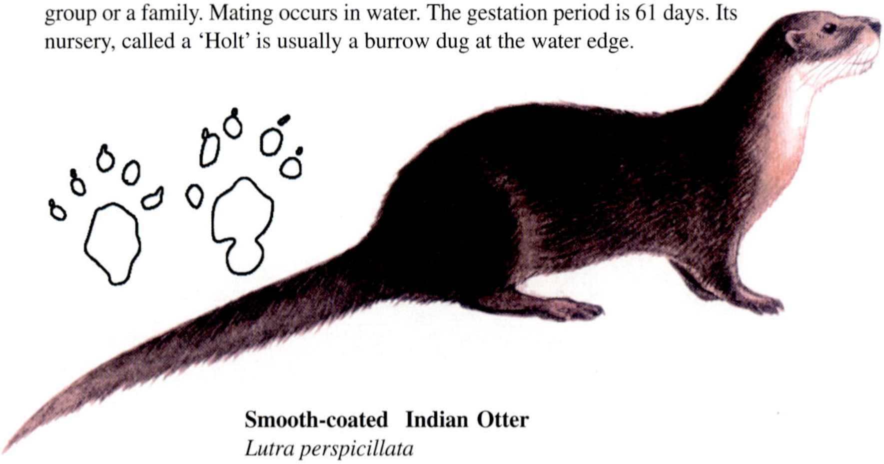

Smooth-coated Indian Otter

Lutra perspicillata

Local names: Neeti Kukka (Telugu), Ludra, Jal manus (Hindi).

The smooth-coated Indian otter is a short and stout animal with short, smooth and sleek coat which is usually blackish to rufous chocolate brown in colour, or sometimes sandy or tawny brown. It can be distinguished from the common otter by the following characters- it is usually smaller in size, the dorsal fur of its coat is not grizzled and the white on the underparts is restricted to the cheeks and throat and does not extend below the chest. It has a large skull and teeth. The head and body measures 65-75 cm, while the tail is 40-45 cm long. It weighs 7-11 kg. It occupies the margins of lakes, streams, large canals and tanks. It mainly feeds on fish and other aquatic animals. When the streams dry up, it resorts to hunting smaller animals in jungles. It gives out a yelp or a whistle like alarm call when excited. Little is known about its breeding habits.

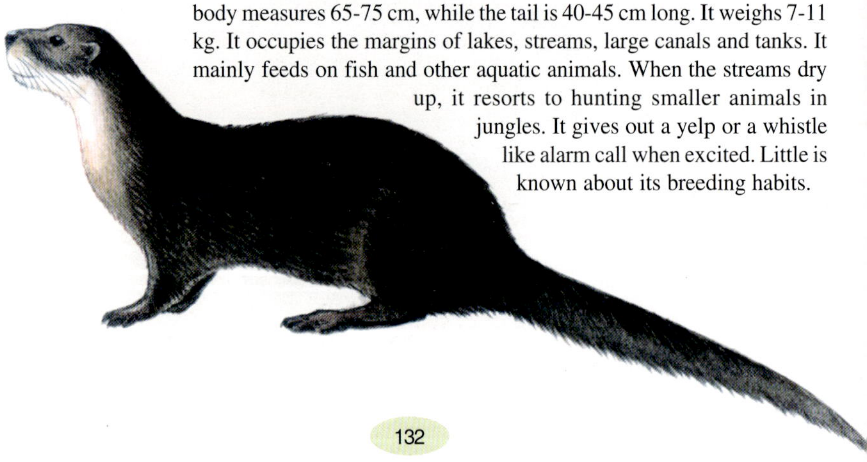

Small Indian Civet or Civet Cat

Viverricula indica

Local Names: Punuga Pilli (Telugu), Kasturi (Hindi)

The civet is a grayish brown animal, no bigger than a domestic cat, with short legs, small, rounded ears, and a very long tail that is ringed with black and white. The coat is striped and spotted lengthwise with black. The neck has cross bars. It measures 90 cm in entire length, of which the tail is 30 cm long and weighs 3-4 kg.

The civet cat inhabits long grass or scrub forests where it usually lives in holes under the rocks or under bushes. It searches for food on the ground at nights. Food consists of rats, squirrels, poultry, small birds, lizards and insects. It also feeds on fruits, roots and other vegetable matter. It can climb a vertical tree with ease, and often does so in search of food. It leads a solitary life and is seldom seen in pairs. About 4-5 young ones are born in a litter. The mother alone cares for the young. 'Civet' is a musky scent extracted from the scent glands of this animal.

Common Palm Civet or Toddy Cat

Paradoxurus hermaphroditus

Local names: Manu Pilli (Telugu), Lakati, Khatas, Menuri (Hindi).

The toddy cat is a short legged animal with coarse, greyish-black fur with a pattern of black longitudinal stripes on the back. It has a long, furry black-tipped tail , a black forehead and chin and greyish black cheeks. There are white patches under the eyes. The limbs, particularly the forelimbs, are dark brown or black. Its body is 60 cm in length while the tail measures another 60 cm. It can weigh 2.7-4.5 kg.

It inhabits well-wooded regions,and lives in trees. It hunts for food at night. Food consists of birds, smaller mammals as well as fruits. About 3-4 young ones are produced in a litter. Breeding takes place throughout the year.

Indian Hare or Black Naped Hare

Lepus nigricollis

Local names: Kundelu, Chevula Pilli (Telugu), Khargosh (Hindi)

This nocturnal creature has large ears, prominent eyes, coarse fur, and a distinct black or dark brown patch on the back of its neck from ear to shoulder. Its short, blunt tail is tipped black on the upper side.The coat is rufous brown or light brown. Underparts are whitish. The black naped hare has an average body length of 40-50 cm in length and weighs 2-2.3 kg.

It inhabits bushes, grasslands and jungles alternating with cultivated plains. It mostly eats grass. The chief predators of black naped hare are wild cats, dogs, foxes, mongooses, etc. Breeding takes place between October and February. 1-2 young ones are produced in each litter.

Ground Shrew or Grey Musk Shrew

Suncus murinus

Local names: Chuncheluka (Telugu), Chuchunder (Hindi)

The ground shrew is distinguished from an ordinary rat by its long pointed snout, very small eyes, comparatively short tail, small rounded ears, and soft fur which is pale grey or brown in colour. The snout, ears, feet and tail are flesh-pink with scanty hair growth. It grows 15 cm in body length with an 8 cm long tail. It emanates a strong smell of musk. This secretion is produced in greater abundance during the mating season. This nocturnal animal is useful to mankind, because it preys on pestilential insects and rodents. It is commonly found near human habitation. Breeding commences from the juvenile stage itself. 2-3 young ones are born at a time.

Indian Giant Squirrel
Ratufa indica

Local name: Pedda Udutha (Telugu), Karrat, Rasu (Hindi).

This large squirrel has a colourful coat in three shades- bright brown, dark brown limbs and buff. It has light brown eyes, tufted ears, and a flesh coloured snub nose. The face, underparts and the paws are whitish or buff coloured. Tail is red, black or buff coloured. Its body is 50 cm and tail is almost 30 cm long. It is found in the mixed deciduous, moist deciduous and evergreen forests. It is arboreal in habitat. Its food mainly consists of fruits, nuts, bark, gum, insects, etc. The large globular nest is built in trees using twigs, and leaves. They produce loud rattling sound and raise a general alarm (like monkeys) upon sighting any unfamiliar object.

Three Striped Palm Squirrel

Funambulus palmaram

Local names: Udutha (Telugu),Gileheri (Hindi).

This squirrel is commonly seen in gardens and near human settlements. It has a brownish-grey coat with three cream coloured stripes on its back, extending from neck to rump. Underparts are whitish, the tail is grizzled. Its body is 15 cm in length and tail is 18 cm long. Apart from forests, it lives in and around human dwellings, fields, gardens and houses. This noisy creature produces a shrill bird-like call, accompanied by quick jerks of its tail. It feeds on fruits, nuts, buds, bark, pods, young shoots, etc, thereby facilitating pollination. It also eats bird eggs. The female builds nests in the holes of trees or houses, using leaves and grass. The gestation period is 6 weeks. Around 2-3 blind, helpless young ones are produced at a time.

Indian Porcupine

Hystrix indica

Local names: Mulla Pandi, Yedu (Telugu), Sayal (Hindi)

This moderately large rodent, 70-90 cm in length, is easily recognized by its sharp, long quills (hair modified into spines). Each quill measures 15 – 30 cm and has alternate white and black (or dark brown) transverse rings. It weighs 11-18 kg. Although its favorite haunt is the rocky hillsides, it also inhabits both open land and forest areas, living in burrows and caves. Its food mainly consists of grains, roots, fruits and vegetables. It also has the habit of gnawing bones and dropped deer antlers. This suffices the body's calcium requirement and is utilized for the growth of quills. When alarmed, it erects its quills and rattles the hollow tail quills. It is known to rush backwards at a great speed and dash its hind quarters against the enemy, thereby driving its quills deep into its enemy's body. The quills so damaged are dislodged and replaced with new quills. The mother gives birth to 2-4 offsprings. The young ones are born with open eyes and soft short spines over the body. Both parents look after the young ones.

Common House Rat
Rattus rattus

Local names: Yeluka (Telugu), Chuha, Musa, Kala-Mus, Kala Chuha (Hindi).

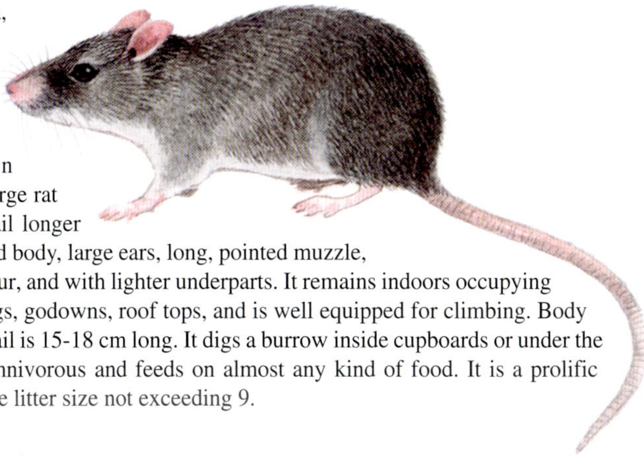

The common house rat is a large rat with a naked tail longer than its head and body, large ears, long, pointed muzzle, long brownish fur, and with lighter underparts. It remains indoors occupying houses, buildings, godowns, roof tops, and is well equipped for climbing. Body is 10 cm long, tail is 15-18 cm long. It digs a burrow inside cupboards or under the ground. It is omnivorous and feeds on almost any kind of food. It is a prolific breeder, with the litter size not exceeding 9.

Common House Mouse
Mus musculus

Local Names: Chuhi, Musi, Mesuri

It is a medium sized mouse with large ears and a dark tail, which is longer than the body. Its coat has short and soft fur and is brown above and greyish white below. It measures about 5-8 cm in body length and the tail is about 10 cm long. It lives in houses, gardens, and fields. It climbs well and usually follows a single route daily. It is omnivorous and feeds on almost any kind of food. The nest is built out of soft material in tiny crevices and recesses. It is a prolific breeder, breeding 3-5 times per year and producing 4-8 blind young ones in each litter. These young ones attain quick maturity and are capable of producing young ones as soon as they are just one month old.

Indian Flying Fox or Indian Fruit Bat

Pteropus giganteus

Local names: Sikurayi, Gabbilam (Telugu), Gadal, Badur, Chamgadad (Hindi).

The flying fox is the largest bat in India. Its body length is 23 cm, wingspan can be upto 1.3 m. It weighs 565-625 g. This short-tailed, fox-headed bat has a reddish brown, furry body, small rounded ears, black wings, blackish snout and dark brown eyes. It is pale brown on the hind neck and shoulders. It flies with slow wing beats. It roosts during the day in large, noisy colonies on trees. After sunset, it feeds mainly on fruits and the colony is very destructive in orchards. It breeds once a year, giving birth to one offspring in early February after a gestation period of 140-150 days. The female carries its young one in flight.

Fulvous Fruit-Bat

Rousettus leschenaulti

Local Name: Gabbilam (Telugu)

This medium sized bat has a dull yellowish grey or yellowish brown coat and a grey belly. Its body measures 10 cm and tail grows to 2 cm. Fulvous fruit bats live in noisy colonies of 10-2000, often occupying caves, tunnels, old ruins and big trees. The colony smells of fermented fruit, since fruit is this bat's favourite food. It has a very strong sense of smell and a strong memory. Pink coloured, naked young ones are born during two birth peaks, one in March and the other in August. The mother carries the young ones during her nocturnal flight.

Indian False Vampire

Megaderma lyra

Local Name: Not known

This large, well-built tailless bat has an ashy grey or slaty grey furry body, pale underparts, and large rounded ears that are united for one-third of their length. It inhabits old buildings, caves and wells during daytime. It is a carnivore that mainly feeds on large insects such as grasshoppers, moths, and smaller vertebrates like small bats, birds, lizards, frogs, geckos, rats and fish. It flies low, picking up its prey from the ground. Mating takes place in October and November.The young ones are born in late April. The mother carries the young ones during her nocturnal flights.

LIST OF IMPORTANT WILDLIFE NGOS IN ANDHRA PRADESH

(This list is not exhaustive, but gives a fair representation of NGOs working for protecting wildlife across the state)

World Wide Fund for Nature-India A.P. State Office
818, Road No. 2, Castle Hills,
Near NMDC, Masab Tank,
Hyderabad- 500 057
apso@wwfindia.net

Andhra Pradesh Natural History Society
11-2-6, Dasapalla Hills,
Visakhapatnam-530 003
Ph. 0891 563682

Birdwatchers Society of Andhra Pradesh
2/B Atlas Apartments, Road No 10,
Banjara Hills, Hyderabad-500 034
sirajtaher@rediffmail.com
040-2661 2608

Dolphin Nature Conservation Society
54-12-26/2, Vidya Nagar,H. B. Colony
Vsakhapatnam- 22
lovenature@sifymail.com

Nallamalai Foundation
1, Old Block, Samrat Complex,
Saifabad, Hyderabad 500 004
nalfound@eth.net
040- 5575 1436, 2156 1390

NATIONAL AGENCIES FOR WILDLIFE CONSERVATION

World Wide Fund for Nature-India
172B, Lodi Estate, New Delhi -110003
011-51504815-18
www.wwfindia.org

Bombay Natural History Society
Hornbill House
Opposite Lion Gate
Shahid Bhagat Singh Road
Mumbai- 400 023
bnhs@bom4.vsnl.net.in

Wildlife Trust of India
PO Box 3150, New Delhi- 110003.
Ph.011 26326025.

Wildlife Institute of India
Post Bag No. 18, Chandrabani,
Dehradun- 248001, Uttaranchal, India
Ph. 0135 2640111-15
Website: www.wii.gov.in

Wildlife Protection Society of India
S-25, Pancheel Park, New Delhi 110017
Ph: 011-41635920/21 Fax: 41635924
www.wpsi-india.org

Wildlife (Protection) Act 1972 & IUCN Red List simplified – Threatened Birds and Mammals in Andhra Pradesh

In order to provide protection to certain plants and animals in our country, the Wildlife (Protection) Act was passed in the year 1972. This act ensures the ecological and environmental security of our country. Species have been listed in schedules in the Act as per their population status.

The Act states that all wild animals in the country are Government property. No person shall hunt any wild animal specified in Schedule, I, II, III and IV except as provided below. "Hunting" includes capturing, killing, poisoning, snaring and trapping, injuring, destroying or taking any part of the body of any wild animal. In the case of wild birds or reptiles, damaging or disturbing the eggs or nests is also included in hunting.

The Chief Wildlife Warden (CWW) may grant a written permit for special purposes such as education, scientific research, scientific management, collection of specimens for recognised zoos or museums. Such permissions are not granted for species listed in the schedule without prior permission of the Central Government. Of course, permission may be granted for putting down an animal that has become dangerous to human life or is so disabled or diseased as to be beyond recovery, or in self-defence. The killing or wounding in good faith of any wild animal in self-defence or in defence of any other person is not considered to be an offence. If any wild animal is killed or wounded in defence of a person, its body is considered to be government property.

Without a certificate of ownership or previous permission of the CWW, nobody is permitted to sell, transfer or gift any wild or captive animal, animal article, trophy or meat of an animal mentioned in Schedule I or Part II of Schedule II. Let's take a look at what each schedule implies:

Schedule-I

This schedule contains the list of the **most endangered species** of animals in India.

No person can hunt any animal mentioned in this schedule. However, the Chief Wildlife Warden may give permission to hunt such an animal if he is satisfied that the animal has become dangerous to human life or is so disabled or diseased as to be beyond recovery. The permission has to be in written form with the reasons stated. This procedure applies to all the schedules.

Schedule-II

This schedule also contains a list of **endangered wild animals**. However they are less endangered in comparison to the animals in Schedule I. The animals mentioned in this schedule and the ones following it may be killed if they pose a threat to standing crops.

Schedule-III

This schedule contains a list of endangered animals that follow Schedule II in importance.

Schedule –IV

The species listed under this schedule are considered to be of lesser conservational importance than those in Schedule III. However the same penalties apply for hunting animals in this schedule.

Schedule-V

Any animal except the ones mentioned in Schedule I and part II of Schedule II may be termed vermin by the Central Government for a specific area, for a specified period of time if it is found to be creating a nuisance.

IUCN Redlist

The Red List is based on information supplied by IUCN's Species Survival Commission (SSC), a network of 7,000 experts on plants, animals and conservation issues, and from data provided by a number of partner organizations. All bird data is supplied by BirdLife International. Collectively, the SSC network holds what is the most complete scientific knowledge base on the biology and current conservation status of species.

Major analyses of the Red List were produced in 1996 and 2000. The 1996 List revealed that one in four mammal species and one in eight bird species faces extinction, while the 2000 List confirmed that the global extinction crisis is as bad or worse than believed. Dramatic declines were reported in populations of many species, including reptiles and primates.

There are seven aspects considered for categorizing species in 'Global Threatened Categories' viz., extent of occurrence, suspected change in population in the last 20 years, habitat fragmentation, habitat condition, habitat status, human impact and the intrinsic capacity to adapt.

IUCN has assigned the following categories and criteria for threatened species:

Extinct (X): A taxon is extinct when there is no reasonable doubt that the last individual has died.

Extinct in wild (EW): This category is for taxa presumed to be extinct in the wild, and is known to be surviving only in cultivation, captivity or in a population far away from its home range.

Critically Endangered (CR): A taxon is critically endangered when it is facing an extremely high risk of extinction in the wild in the immediate future.

Endangered (EN): A taxon is endangered when it is not critically endangered but is facing a high risk of extinction in the wild in the near future.

Vulnerable (VU): A taxon is vulnerable when it faces a high risk of extinction in the wild in the medium term future.

Lower Risk (LR): A taxon is Lower Risk when it has been evaluated, does not satisfy the criteria for any of the categories- CR, EN or VU.

Data Deficient (DD): A taxon is data deficient when there is inadequate information to make a direct, or indirect assessment of its risk of extinction. Even though information is available about the species habits and habitat, insufficient information about its distribution and population status could put the taxon in the DD category. Hence, DD is not a category of risk.

Conservation Importance of Birds and Mammals described in this book

COMMON NAME	SCIENTIFIC NAME	I-WPA	IUCN Red List 2004
Barbet, Crimsonbreasted	*Megalaima haemacephala*	*Schedule IV*	
Barbet, Large Green	*Megalaima zeylanica*	*Schedule IV*	
Cuckoo, Common Hawk	*Cuculus varius*	*Schedule IV*	
Cuckoo, Pied Crested	*Clamator jacobinus*	*Schedule IV*	
Cuckoo,Plaintive	*Cacomantis passerinus*	*Schedule IV*	
Drongo, Black	*Dicrurus adsimilis*	*Schedule IV*	
Drongo, Racket tailed	*Dicrurus paradiseus*	*Schedule IV*	
Malkoha,Small Greenbilled	*Phaenicophaeus viridirostris*	*Schedule IV*	
Barheaded Goose	*Anser indicus*	*Schedule IV*	
Blackwinged Stilt	*Himantopus himantopus*	*Schedule IV*	
Blue Rock Pigeon	*Columba livia*	*Schedule IV*	
Brahminy Duck	*Tadorna ferruginea*	*Schedule IV*	
Bunting	*Emberiza bruniceps*	*Schedule IV*	
Cattle Egret	*Bubulcus ibis*	*Schedule IV*	
Comb Duck	*Sarkidiornis melanotos*	*Schedule IV*	
Common Mongoose	*Herpestes edwardsi*	*Schedule II Pt II*	
Coot	*Fulica atra*	*Schedule IV*	
Cotton Teal	*Nettapus coromandelianus*	*Schedule IV*	
Crow Pheasant	*Centropus sinensis*	*Schedule IV*	
Darter	*Anhinga rufa*	*Schedule IV*	
Emerald Dove	*Chalcophaps indica*	*Schedule IV*	
Grey Heron	*Ardea cinerea*	*Schedule IV*	
Indian Hare (Black Naped Hare)	*Lepus nigricollis*	*Schedule IV*	
Jungle Babbler	*Turdoides striatus*	*Schedule IV*	
Kestrel	*Falco tinnunculus*	*Schedule IV*	
Koel, Asian	*Eudynamys scolopacea*	*Schedule IV*	
Large Grey Babbler	*Turdoides malcolmi*	*Schedule IV*	
Lesser Whistling Teal	*Dendrocygna javanica*	*Schedule IV*	
Little Brown Dove	*Streptopelia senegalensis*	*Schedule IV*	
Little Cormorant	*Phalacrocorax niger*	*Schedule IV*	
Little Egret	*Egretta garzetta*	*Schedule IV*	
Night Heron	*Nycticorax nycticorax*	*Schedule IV*	
Owl, Barn	*Tyto alba*	*Schedule I*	
Owl, Great Horned	*Bubo bubo*	*Schedule I*	
Owl, Spotted	*Athene brama*	*Schedule I*	
Pond Heron	*Ardeola grayii*	*Schedule IV*	
Purple Heron	*Ardea purpurea*	*Schedule IV*	
Rain Quail	*Coturnix coromandelica*	*Schedule IV*	
Red Whiskered Bulbul	*Pycnonotus jocosus*	*Schedule IV*	
Redcrested Pochard	*Netta rufina*	*Schedule IV*	
Red-vented Bulbul	*Pycnonotus cafer*	*Schedule IV*	
Ring Dove	*Streptopelia decaocto*	*Schedule IV*	
Shoveller	*Anas clypeata*	*Schedule IV*	
Spotbill Duck	*Anas poecilorhyncha*	*Schedule IV*	
Spotted Dove	*Streptopelia chinensis*	*Schedule IV*	
Stone Curlew	*Burhinus oedicnemus*	*Schedule IV*	
The Indian Porcupine	*Hystrix indica*	*Schedule IV*	
Whitebrowed Bulbul	*Pycnonotus luteolus*	*Schedule IV*	

COMMON NAME	SCIENTIFIC NAME	I-WPA	IUCN Red List 2004
Whiteheaded Babbler	*Turdoides affinis*	*Schedule IV*	
Yellow footed Green Pigeon	*Treron phoenicopterus*	*Schedule IV*	
Yelloweyed Babbler	*Chrysomma sinense*	*Schedule IV*	
Crow, House	*Corvus splendens*	*Schedule V*	
Fruit Bat	*Rousettus leschenaulti*	*Schedule V*	
Crow, Jungle	*Corvus macrorhynchos*	*Schedule V*	
Pie, Indian Tree	*Dendrocitta vagabunda*	*Schedule IV*	
Lesser Flamingo	*Phoeniconaias minor*	*Schedule IV*	NT
Painted Stork	*Mycteria leucocephala*	*Schedule IV*	NT
Spot billed Pelican	*Pelecanus philippensis*	*Schedule IV*	VU A2cde+3cde
Slender Loris	*Loris targigradus*	*Schedule I Part I*	NT
White-backed Vulture	*Gyps bengalensis*	*Schedule I Part III*	CR A2ce+3ce
Gaur (Indian Bison)	*Bos gaurus*	*Schedule I Part I*	
Blackbuck (Indian Antelope)	*Antilope cervicapra*	*Schedule I Part I*	V
Chinkara (Indian Gazelle)	*Gazella gazella*	*Schedule I Part I*	
Fishing Cat	*Felis viverrina*	*Schedule I Part I*	
Four Horned Antelope (Chowsingha)	*Tetracerus quadricornis*	*Schedule I Part I*	V
Indian Chevrotain (Mouse Deer)	*Tragulus mimenna*	*Schedule I Part I*	
Indian Elephant	*Elephas maximus*	*Schedule I Part I*	E
Leopard (Panther)	*Panthera pardus*	*Schedule I Part I*	
Leopard-Cat	*Felis bengalensis*	*Schedule I Part I*	
Sloth Bear	*Melursus ursinus*	*Schedule I Part I*	
Tiger	*Panthera tigris*	*Schedule I Part I*	E
Wolf	*Canis lupus*	*Schedule I Part I*	
Great Indian Bustard	*Ardeotis nigriceps*	*Schedule I Part III*	EN C2a(ii)
Lesser Florican	*Sypheotides indica*	*Schedule I Part III*	EN A3bc; C1
Osprey	*Pandion haliaetus*	*Schedule I Part III*	
Rhesus Macaque	*Macaca mulatta*	*Schedule II Part I*	
Bonnet Macaque	*Macaca radiata*	*Schedule II Part I*	
Common Langur	*Semnopithecus entellus*	*Schedule II Part I*	
Common Palm Civet	*Paradoxurus hermaphroditus*	*Schedule II Part II*	
Dhole (Indian Wild Dog)	*Cuon alpinus*	*Schedule II Part I*	EN C2a(i)
Giant Squirrel	*Ratufa indica*	*Schedule II Part I*	V
Indian Fox	*Vulpes bengalensis*	*Schedule II Part I*	
Jackal	*Canis aureus*	*Schedule II Part II*	
Jungle Cat	*Felis chaus*	*Schedule II Part II*	
Otter, Common	*Lutra lutra*	*Schedule II Part II*	NT
Otter, Indian Smooth-coated	*Lutrogale perspicillata*	*Schedule II Part II*	VU A2acd
Small Indian Civet	*Viverricula indica*	*Schedule II Part II*	
Chital (Spotted Deer)	*Axis axis*	*Schedule III*	
Indian Wild Boar	*Sus scrofa*	*Schedule III*	
Muntjac (Barking Deer)	*Muntiacus muntjac*	*Schedule III*	
Nilgai (Blue Bull)	*Boselaphus tragocamelus*	*Schedule III*	
Sambar	*Cervus unicolor*	*Schedule III*	
Striped Hyena	*Hyaena hyaena*	*Schedule III*	

CHECKLIST OF BIRDS FROM A FEW PROTECTED AREAS OF ANDHRA PRADESH

	Little Grebe	Spot billed Pelican	Little Cormorant	Darter	Cattle Egret	Little Egret	Grey Heron	Night Heron	Pond Heron	Purple Heron	Openbilled Stork	Painted Stork	Whitenecked Stork	Black Ibis	White Ibis	Eurasian Spoonbill	Lesser Flamingo	Greater Flamingo	Brahminy Duck	Comb Duck	Spotbill Duck	Redcrested Pochard
Nehru Zoo			✓	✓	✓	✓	✓	✓	✓	✓	✓	✓	✓		✓		✓		✓	✓	✓	✓
Sanjeevaiah Park			✓		✓	✓	✓	✓	✓	✓		✓			✓	✓					✓	
Shameerpet	✓	✓	✓		✓																	
Anantgiri	✓		✓		✓	✓	✓		✓	✓	✓	✓	✓	✓	✓				✓	✓	✓	✓
ICRISAT		✓	✓	✓	✓	✓	✓	✓	✓	✓	✓		✓	✓					✓	✓		
Mriguvani National Park			✓	✓	✓	✓	✓	✓	✓	✓	✓	✓							✓		✓	✓
KBR National Park	✓		✓		✓	✓	✓	✓	✓	✓											✓	
Manjeera Bird Sanctuary		✓	✓	✓	✓	✓	✓	✓	✓	✓	✓	✓	✓	✓	✓	✓				✓		
Rollapadu Sanctuary	✓	✓	✓	✓	✓	✓	✓		✓	✓	✓	✓	✓		✓	✓		✓	✓	✓	✓	✓
NSTR			✓		✓	✓	✓	✓	✓	✓	✓	✓	✓	✓	✓	✓						
Pulicat Lake	✓	✓	✓		✓	✓	✓	✓	✓	✓	✓	✓	✓	✓	✓	✓			✓	✓	✓	✓
Uppalapadu Lake	✓	✓	✓		✓	✓	✓	✓	✓	✓	✓	✓			✓	✓					✓	
Kolleru Lake	✓	✓	✓	✓	✓	✓	✓	✓	✓	✓	✓	✓	✓	✓	✓	✓				✓	✓	

	Shoveller	Cotton Teal	Lesser Whistling Teal	Barheaded Goose	Pintail	Crested Hawk Eagle	Crested Serpent Eagle	Short-toed Eagle	Marsh Harrier	Montagu's Harrier	Blackshouldered Kite	Brahminy Kite	Black Kite	Shikra	Scavenger Vulture	Whitebacked Vulture	Osprey	Falcon	Kestrel	Grey Partridge	Painted Partridge	Peafowl
Nehru Zoo	✓	✓	✓					✓	✓		✓	✓	✓	✓	✓	✓			✓	✓		✓
Sanjeevaiah Park	✓	✓	✓								✓	✓	✓	✓			✓	✓	✓	✓		
Shameerpet	✓	✓	✓	✓				✓	✓	✓	✓	✓	✓	✓	✓	✓	✓	✓	✓	✓	✓	✓
Anantgiri	✓	✓	✓			✓	✓	✓	✓	✓	✓	✓	✓	✓		✓			✓	✓		✓
ICRISAT	✓	✓	✓	✓	✓	✓	✓	✓	✓	✓	✓	✓	✓	✓	✓	✓	✓	✓	✓	✓	✓	✓
Mriguvani National Park		✓	✓	✓		✓	✓	✓	✓	✓	✓	✓	✓	✓	✓	✓	✓	✓	✓	✓	✓	✓
KBR National Park											✓	✓	✓	✓				✓	✓	✓	✓	✓
Manjeera Bird Sanctuary	✓	✓	✓	✓	✓		✓	✓	✓	✓	✓	✓	✓	✓	✓	✓	✓		✓	✓		✓
Rollapadu Sanctuary	✓	✓	✓	✓	✓		✓	✓	✓	✓	✓	✓	✓	✓	✓	✓		✓	✓	✓	✓	✓
NSTR	✓	✓	✓	✓	✓	✓	✓	✓	✓	✓	✓	✓	✓	✓	✓	✓	✓	✓	✓	✓	✓	✓
Pulicat Lake	✓	✓	✓		✓				✓	✓	✓	✓	✓	✓			✓		✓			
Uppalapadu Lake	✓	✓							✓		✓	✓	✓	✓					✓			
Kolleru Lake	✓	✓	✓		✓	✓	✓		✓		✓	✓	✓	✓		✓	✓		✓	✓		

	Grey Jungle Fowl	Rain Quail	Coot	Whitebreasted Waterhen	Purple Moorhen	Indian Moorhen	Great Indian Bustard	Lesser Florican	Bronzewinged Jacana	Pheasant-tailed Jacana	Little Ringed Plover	Redwattled Lapwing	Yellowwattled Lapwing	Stone Curlew	Common Sandpiper	Spotted Sandpiper	Little Stint	Common Snipe	Redshank	Blackwinged Stilt	Small Indian Pratincole	Blackheaded Gull	Brownheaded Gull
Nehru Zoo			✓	✓	✓	✓			✓	✓	✓	✓		✓	✓	✓	✓			✓	✓	✓	
Sanjeevaiah Park			✓	✓	✓	✓			✓	✓	✓	✓		✓		✓	✓	✓		✓		✓	✓
Shameerpet		✓	✓	✓	✓	✓			✓	✓	✓	✓	✓	✓	✓	✓	✓	✓	✓	✓	✓	✓	✓
Anantgiri		✓	✓									✓	✓	✓			✓			✓			
ICRISAT		✓	✓	✓	✓	✓			✓	✓		✓	✓	✓	✓	✓	✓	✓	✓	✓	✓		✓
Mriguvani National Park		✓	✓	✓	✓				✓	✓		✓	✓	✓						✓			
KBR National Park		✓	✓	✓					✓	✓		✓	✓	✓	✓	✓				✓			
Manjeera Bird Sanctuary		✓	✓	✓	✓	✓			✓	✓	✓	✓	✓	✓	✓	✓	✓	✓	✓	✓		✓	✓
Rollapadu Sanctuary		✓	✓	✓	✓	✓	✓	✓	✓	✓	✓	✓	✓	✓	✓	✓	✓	✓	✓	✓	✓	✓	✓
NSTR	✓	✓	✓	✓	✓	✓			✓	✓		✓	✓	✓		✓	✓	✓	✓	✓		✓	✓
Pulicat Lake			✓	✓	✓	✓						✓				✓	✓	✓	✓	✓		✓	✓
Uppalapadu Lake			✓	✓	✓	✓			✓	✓		✓			✓	✓	✓	✓	✓	✓		✓	✓
Kolleru Lake			✓	✓	✓	✓			✓	✓		✓		✓		✓	✓	✓	✓	✓		✓	✓

	Indian River Tern	Common Sandgrouse	Little Brown Dove	Ring Dove	Spotted Dove	Blue Rock Pigeon	Green Pigeon	Emerald Dove	Blossomheaded Parakeet	Roseringed Parakeet	Crow Pheasant	Common Hawk Cuckoo	Pied Crested Cuckoo	Plaintive Cuckoo	Small Greenbilled Malkoha	Asian Koel	Barn Owl	Spotted Owlet	Great Horned Owl	Common Indian Nightjar	House Swift	Palm Swift
Nehru Zoo	✓		✓		✓	✓			✓	✓	✓	✓	✓	✓	✓	✓	✓	✓		✓	✓	✓
Sanjeevaiah Park	✓		✓		✓	✓			✓	✓	✓	✓		✓		✓	✓	✓			✓	✓
Shameerpet	✓	✓	✓	✓	✓	✓			✓	✓	✓	✓		✓	✓	✓	✓	✓	✓	✓	✓	✓
Anantgiri		✓	✓	✓	✓	✓	✓	✓	✓	✓	✓	✓	✓	✓	✓	✓	✓	✓	✓	✓	✓	✓
ICRISAT	✓	✓	✓	✓	✓	✓	✓		✓	✓	✓	✓	✓	✓	✓	✓	✓	✓	✓	✓	✓	✓
Mriguvani National Park	✓	✓	✓	✓	✓	✓			✓	✓	✓	✓	✓	✓	✓	✓	✓	✓	✓	✓	✓	✓
KBR National Park	✓	✓	✓	✓	✓	✓			✓	✓	✓	✓	✓	✓	✓	✓	✓	✓	✓	✓	✓	✓
Manjeera Bird Sanctuary	✓	✓	✓	✓	✓	✓			✓	✓	✓	✓	✓	✓	✓	✓	✓	✓	✓	✓	✓	✓
Rollapadu Sanctuary	✓	✓	✓	✓	✓	✓			✓	✓	✓	✓	✓	✓	✓	✓	✓	✓	✓	✓	✓	✓
NSTR	✓	✓	✓	✓	✓	✓	✓	✓	✓	✓	✓	✓	✓	✓	✓	✓	✓	✓	✓	✓	✓	✓
Pulicat Lake	✓		✓		✓	✓				✓					✓	✓		✓				✓
Uppalapadu Lake	✓		✓		✓	✓				✓	✓					✓		✓			✓	✓
Kolleru Lake	✓		✓	✓		✓			✓	✓	✓	✓	✓	✓		✓		✓			✓	✓

	Kolleru Lake	Uppalapadu Lake	Pulicat Lake	NSTR	Rollapadu Sanctuary	Manjeera Bird Sanctuary	KBR National Park	Mriguvani National Park	ICRISAT	Anantgiri	Shameerpet	Sanjeevaiah Park	Nehru Zoo
Pied Kingfisher	✓	✓	✓	✓	✓	✓	✓	✓	✓	✓	✓	✓	✓
Small Blue Kingfisher	✓	✓	✓	✓	✓	✓	✓	✓	✓	✓	✓	✓	✓
Whitebreasted Kingfisher	✓	✓	✓	✓	✓	✓	✓	✓	✓	✓	✓	✓	✓
Bluetailed Bee-Eater	✓			✓	✓	✓	✓	✓	✓	✓	✓		✓
Small Green Bee-Eater	✓	✓	✓	✓	✓	✓	✓	✓		✓	✓	✓	✓
Indian Roller	✓	✓	✓	✓	✓	✓	✓	✓	✓	✓	✓	✓	✓
Hoopoe	✓	✓	✓	✓	✓	✓	✓	✓	✓	✓	✓	✓	✓
Grey Hornbill	✓			✓	✓	✓	✓	✓	✓	✓	✓	✓	
Large Green Barbet				✓						✓			
Coppersmith Barbet	✓	✓	✓	✓	✓	✓	✓	✓	✓	✓	✓	✓	✓
Goldenbacked Woodpecker	✓	✓	✓	✓	✓	✓	✓	✓	✓	✓	✓	✓	✓
Pygmy Woodpecker	✓			✓						✓			
Ashycrowned Finch Lark	✓	✓	✓	✓	✓	✓	✓	✓	✓	✓	✓		✓
Redwinged Bush Lark				✓	✓	✓		✓	✓	✓	✓		✓
Rufoustailed Finch Lark				✓	✓	✓	✓	✓	✓	✓	✓		✓
Dusky Crag Martin	✓	✓	✓	✓	✓	✓	✓	✓	✓	✓	✓	✓	✓
Common Swallow	✓	✓	✓	✓	✓	✓	✓	✓	✓	✓	✓	✓	✓
Redrumped Swallow	✓	✓	✓	✓	✓	✓	✓	✓	✓	✓	✓	✓	✓
Wiretailed Swallow	✓	✓	✓	✓	✓	✓	✓		✓		✓		
Paddyfield Pipit				✓	✓	✓			✓	✓	✓		✓
Grey Wagtail	✓	✓	✓	✓	✓	✓	✓	✓	✓	✓	✓	✓	✓
Large Pied Wagtail	✓	✓	✓	✓	✓	✓	✓	✓	✓	✓	✓	✓	✓

	Small Minivet	Scarlet Minivet	Redvented Bulbul	Whitebrowed Bulbul	Red Whiskered Bulbul	Common Iora	Grey Shrike	Rufousbacked Shrike	Bluethroat	Pied Bush Chat	Stone Chat	Black Redstart	Indian Robin	Magpie-Robin	Blue Rock Thrush	Jungle Babbler	Large Grey Babbler	Whiteheaded Babbler	Yelloweyed Babbler	Ashy Prinia	Tailor Bird	Tickell's Blue Flycatcher
Nehru Zoo	✓		✓			✓		✓	✓	✓	✓	✓	✓	✓	✓	✓	✓	✓		✓	✓	✓
Sanjeevaiah Park			✓			✓		✓		✓		✓	✓	✓	✓	✓	✓	✓		✓	✓	✓
Shameerpet			✓			✓		✓		✓	✓	✓	✓	✓	✓	✓	✓	✓	✓	✓	✓	
Anantgiri	✓	✓	✓	✓	✓	✓	✓	✓		✓	✓	✓	✓	✓	✓	✓	✓	✓	✓	✓	✓	✓
ICRISAT	✓		✓			✓	✓	✓	✓	✓	✓	✓	✓	✓	✓	✓	✓	✓	✓	✓	✓	
Mriguvani National Park	✓		✓			✓		✓		✓		✓	✓	✓	✓	✓	✓	✓	✓	✓	✓	✓
KBR National Park			✓			✓	✓	✓		✓	✓	✓	✓	✓	✓	✓	✓	✓	✓	✓	✓	
Manjeera Bird Sanctuary			✓	✓		✓	✓	✓	✓	✓	✓	✓	✓	✓	✓	✓	✓	✓	✓	✓	✓	✓
Rollapadu Sanctuary	✓		✓			✓	✓	✓	✓	✓	✓	✓	✓	✓	✓	✓	✓	✓	✓	✓	✓	✓
NSTR	✓	✓	✓	✓	✓	✓	✓	✓	✓	✓	✓	✓	✓	✓	✓	✓	✓	✓	✓	✓	✓	✓
Pulicat Lake			✓			✓	✓	✓		✓			✓	✓		✓	✓	✓		✓	✓	
Uppalapadu Lake			✓			✓	✓	✓		✓			✓	✓		✓	✓	✓		✓	✓	
Kolleru Lake			✓			✓	✓	✓	✓	✓		✓	✓	✓			✓	✓		✓	✓	✓

	Paradise Flycatcher	Whitebrowed Fantail Flycatcher	Tickell's Flowerpecker	Purple Sunbird	Purplerumped Sunbird	Blackheaded Munia	Red Munia	Spotted Munia	Whitethroated Munia	House Sparrow	Yellowthroated Sparrow	Baya	Streaked Weaver	Common Myna	Rosy Pastor	Pied Myna	Hill Myna	Golden Oriole	Black Drongo	Racket tailed Drongo	Ashy Swallow-Shrike	House Crow	Jungle Crow	Indian Tree Pie
Nehru Zoo	✓		✓	✓	✓	✓		✓	✓	✓		✓	✓	✓	✓			✓	✓		✓	✓	✓	✓
Sanjeevaiah Park	✓		✓	✓	✓			✓	✓	✓		✓	✓	✓	✓	✓		✓	✓			✓	✓	✓
Shameerpet			✓	✓	✓	✓	✓	✓	✓	✓		✓		✓	✓			✓	✓		✓	✓	✓	✓
Anantgiri	✓	✓	✓	✓	✓	✓	✓	✓	✓	✓	✓	✓		✓	✓			✓	✓	✓	✓	✓	✓	✓
ICRISAT	✓	✓	✓	✓	✓	✓	✓	✓	✓	✓	✓	✓	✓	✓	✓			✓	✓		✓	✓	✓	✓
Mriguvani National Park	✓	✓	✓	✓	✓		✓	✓	✓	✓		✓		✓	✓			✓	✓		✓	✓	✓	✓
KBR National Park		✓	✓	✓	✓	✓	✓	✓	✓	✓		✓	✓	✓	✓			✓	✓		✓	✓	✓	✓
Manjeera Bird Sanctuary	✓	✓	✓	✓	✓	✓	✓	✓	✓	✓		✓	✓	✓	✓			✓	✓		✓	✓	✓	✓
Rollapadu Sanctuary			✓	✓	✓	✓	✓	✓	✓	✓		✓	✓	✓	✓			✓	✓		✓	✓	✓	✓
NSTR	✓	✓	✓	✓	✓	✓	✓	✓	✓	✓	✓	✓	✓	✓	✓		✓	✓	✓	✓	✓	✓	✓	✓
Pulicat Lake			✓	✓	✓					✓		✓		✓		✓		✓	✓		✓	✓	✓	✓
Uppalapadu Lake			✓	✓	✓					✓		✓		✓		✓		✓	✓		✓	✓	✓	✓
Kolleru Lake	✓		✓	✓	✓			✓		✓		✓	✓	✓	✓		✓	✓	✓		✓	✓	✓	✓

GLOSSARY OF TERMS USED

Aquaculture: The science, art, and business of cultivating marine or freshwater food fish or shellfish, such as oysters, clams, salmon, and trout, under controlled conditions or cultivating aquatic plants for food. Aquafarming.

Backwaters: Water held or pushed back by a dam or current. A body of water that was created by a flood or tide or by being held or forced back by a dam.

Browsing: Feeding off branches, leaves, young shoots, and other vegetation by ungulates (deer, antilopes) .

Carrion: Dead and decaying flesh.

Clavicles: One of the bones of the pectoral girdle in many vertebrates. Equivalent to the collar bone.

Commensal: A species that lives in close association with another speceis without gaining from it or harming it.

Conifers: Needle-leaved or scale-leaved, chiefly evergreen, cone-bearing gymnospermous trees or shrubs such as pines, spruces and firs.

Crustaceans: Aquatic arthropods of the class Crustacea, including lobsters, crabs, shrimps, and barnacles, characteristically having a segmented body, a chitinous exoskeleton, and paired, jointed limbs.

Deciduous: Shedding or losing of foliage by trees at the end of the growing season.

Decimate: To destroy or kill a large part of (a group).

Dimorphism: Two physical forms seen in individuals of the same species.

Dorsal: The back or upper part of an animal.

Estuary: An arm of the sea that extends inland to meet the mouth of a river.

Faecal matter: Animal excreta or bird droppings.

Fetlock: Back of a Horse or Nilgai's leg above the hoof with a tuft of hair.

Flank: The section of flesh on the body of an animal between the last rib and the hip; the side.

Gestation: Pregnancy. The period of development of the foetus in the uterus from conception until birth.

Glutinous tongue: Sticky tongue of the scaly anteater.

Gnawing: To bite, chew on, or erode with the teeth.

Grazing: Feeding on grasses and herbage on ground.

Grizzled: Hair or coat that is grey or streaked with grey.

Hedgerows: A row of bushes, shrubs, or trees forming a hedge.

Herbivore: An animal that feeds chiefly on vegetation.

Heronry: A place where herons nest and breed.

Invertebrate: Lacking a backbone or spinal column; not a vertebrate.

Lagoon: A shallow body of water, especially one separated from a sea by sandbars or coral reefs.

Lichen: A fungus, usually of the class Ascomycetes that grows symbiotically with algae, resulting in a composite organism that characteristically forms a crust-like or branching growth on rocks or tree trunks.

Migratory birds: Birds that move seasonally from one geographic region to another.

Mollusc: An animal having a soft unsegmented body, a mantle, and a protective calcareous shell. e.g. edible shellfish and snails.

Moss: Tiny leafy-stemmed flowerless, nonvascular plants of the class Musci of the division Bryophyta. Mosses grow in patches on damp surfaces.

Offal: Waste parts, especially of a butchered animal.

Omnivore: That which feeds on a variety of animal and plant matter.

Orbitals: Skin around the eye.

Pariah: An untouchable.

Pedicles: A bony base from where antlers arise in deer.

Peninsula: A large mass of land projecting into a body of water, such that it is surrounded by water on three sides.

Perpetuates: Continues indefinitely.

Pied: Black and white.

Pneumatic: Of or relating to air or other gases.

Pollination: To transfer pollen from an anther to the stigma of (a flower).

Prolific breeder: An animal producing offspring in great abundance; fertile.

Pugnacious: Combative in nature; belligerent.

Quill: The hollow stem-like main shaft of a feather. Hard and pointy hair of porcupines and hedgehogs meant for their defence.

Recede: Move back or away from a limit, point, or mark.

Resident birds: Birds that remain in a particular area throughout their lives. Non migratory birds.

Retractile: That can be drawn back or in, such as the claws of a cat.

Rootlets: The thin, small roots or divisions of a root.

Rufous: Orangish brown or brownish orange; reddish.

Ruminant: A hoofed, even-toed, usually horned mammal of the suborder Ruminantia, such as cattle, sheep, goats, deer, and giraffes, characteristically having a stomach divided into four compartments and chewing a cud consisting of regurgitated, partially digested food.

Rut: An annually recurring condition or period of sexual excitement and reproductive activity in male deer.

Scalloped membranes: Membranes with a series of curved projections forming an ornamental border.

Scrubland: An area of land that is uncultivated and covered with sparse stunted vegetation.

Sexual dimorphism: The physical differences between male and female individuals that arise as a consequence of sexual maturation, including the secondary sex characteristics.

Shrub: A woody plant of relatively low

height, having several stems arising from the base and lacking a single trunk. A bush.

Subsonic: Of speeds less than that of sound.

Succulent: Having thick, fleshy, water-storing leaves or stems.

Supercilium: The eyebrow.

Teat: A nipple of the mammary gland.

Terrestrial: Living or growing on land; not aquatic.

Tine: Branch of an antler.

Tragus: The projection of skin-covered cartilage in front of external ear.

Transverse: Situated or lying across; crosswise.

Tuber: Swollen, fleshy, usually underground stem of a plant, such as the potato, bearing buds from which new plant shoots arise.

Tushes: Un-emerged tusks in female elephants and makhna males.

Tusk: An elongated pointed tooth, usually one of a pair, extending outside of the mouth in certain animals such as the walrus, elephant, or wild boar.

Ungulate: Hoofed mammals such as horses, cattle, deer and boar.

Ventral: The underside or front of an animal.

Wattle: A fleshy, wrinkled, often brightly coloured fold of skin hanging from the neck or throat, characteristic of certain birds, such as chickens or turkeys, and some lizards.

Whelp: A young offspring of a mammal, such as a dog or wolf.

Withers: Ridge between a Horse or Nilgai's shoulders, a point from where the animal's height is measured.

INDEX

A

B

C

SUGGESTED READING

ALI, Salim. 2002. *The book of Indian birds*. 13th (Revised) ed. (Series Ed.: DANIEL, J. C.) Mumbai: Bombay Natural History Society. Oxford University Press.

GRIMMETT, Richard, Carol Inskipp, and Tim Inskipp. 1998. *Birds of the Indian Subcontinent.* 1st ed. (With the collaboration of Sarath Kotagama and Shahid Ali.) (Helm Identification Guides.) London: Christopher Helm, A & C Black.

HAWKINS, R. E. (Ed.) 1986. *Encyclopedia of Indian natural history*. (Series Eds.: NORDEN, Doris, and Bittu Sahgal.) Bombay, Delhi, Calcutta, Madras: Bombay Natural History Society & Oxford University Press.

KAZMIERCZAK, Krys. 2000. *A field guide to the birds of India, Sri Lanka, Pakistan, Nepal, Bhutan, Bangladesh and the Maldives.* New Delhi: Om Book Service.

MENON, Vivek, 2003, *A guide to the Mammals of India*. 1st ed.

PRATER, S.H. 1971, *The book of Indian animals.* Third Edition. Bombay Natural History Society. Oxford University Press.

TAHER, Siraj A., and Aasheesh Pittie. 1989. *A checklist of birds of Andhra Pradesh.* Hyderabad, India: Published by the authors.

Tirtsch, Mark F., 2001, *Traveller's guide to Wildlife in India,* 1st ed. Harper Collins, London.

NOTES

NOTES

NOTES

NOTES